MASSASOIT OF THE WAMPANOAGS

MASSASOIT

of the
WAMPANOAGS

WITH A BRIEF COMMENTARY ON INDIAN CHARACTER; AND SKETCHES OF OTHER GREAT CHIEFS, TRIBES AND NATIONS; ALSO A CHAPTER ON SAMOSET, SQUANTO AND HOBAMOCK, THREE EARLY NATIVE FRIENDS OF THE PLYMOUTH COLONISTS

Alvin G. Weeks

Past Great Sachem of the Improved Order of Red Men of Massachusetts and President of the Massasoit Memorial Association

HERITAGE BOOKS
2008

HERITAGE BOOKS

AN IMPRINT OF HERITAGE BOOKS, INC.

Books, CDs, and more—Worldwide

For our listing of thousands of titles see our website
at
www.HeritageBooks.com

A Facsimile Reprint
Published 2008 by
HERITAGE BOOKS, INC.
Publishing Division
100 Railroad Ave. #104
Westminster, Maryland 21157

International Standard Book Numbers
Paperbound: 978-0-7884-2797-8
Clothbound: 978-0-7884-7593-1

FOREWORD

IN the summer of 1910, while serving as Great Sachem of the Improved Order of Red Men of Massachusetts, I had occasion to accompany my Deputy Great Sachem for the Plymouth District and a party of Great Chiefs and members of the order with their families and friends, on a visitation to the tribe located in that old historic town. Our official duties performed, we visited the many places of particular interest, the spots especially consecrated to Freedom by the restless energy of the men of three centuries ago.

We saw the beautiful memorial erected to the Pilgrims, and the memorable rock which their feet first pressed on December 21, 1620; we climbed the hill to view the spot where so many of them were laid at rest during their first winter of hardship and suffering, and where later the ashes of many more were mingled with the dust; we stood on the summit of Cole's Hill from which we looked out upon the harbor where the Mayflower once lay at anchor; we saw the relics of bygone days, exhibited in the Memorial Hall, *and traversed the same old streets laid out by the fathers.*

Many of us had seen it all before, while for others it was the first visit; but, whether for the first time, or to view again and again the old historic spots, the real landmarks of the birthplace of free government, as exemplified by nearly three hundred years of colonial and national life, the patriotic interest and enthusiasm of all alike was thoroughly aroused.

A bronze tablet on a house on Leyden Street, marking the spot where, on March 22, 1621, Massasoit and Governor Carver entered into a treaty of peace, friendship and mutual aid and protection, attracted our attention. I had seen it many times before, but it seemed fraught with a new significance on that occasion. Whether the mental association of the name of our order with the aborigines, or that of my official designation with that of the great chief of the Wampanoags contributed to the thought, I cannot say; but for some reason the suggestion came to my mind that in 1920 the people of Massachusetts undoubtedly would celebrate in fitting manner the third centenary of the landing of the Pilgrim Fathers. In my report at the conclusion of my term in the Great Chieftaincy, I brought this matter to the attention of the Great Council with a recommendation that steps be taken towards erecting, in connection with the celebration of this Centen-

nial, a monument or other memorial to Massasoit, Great Sachem of the Wampanoags, who for forty years religiously observed both the spirit and the letter of the treaty he had made with the colonists, and urged his sons to maintain the same friendly relations. The recommendation was not fruitful of immediate results, but eventually it took root, and, following it, some of the members of the order formed a corporation under the name of the Massasoit Memorial Association, for the purpose of carrying out the project.

Primarily the Improved Order of Red Men is a patriotic society, tracing its descent from the Sons of Liberty, and limiting its membership to American citizens; and, while teaching patriotism, it has endeavored to preserve some of the customs of the aborigines, and to pay due tribute to their many manly virtues, which we, as the dominant race, have been too strongly inclined to overlook or to ignore. In pursuit of this general purpose, and in aid of the project which we have undertaken, this work has been prepared for presentation to those who may desire to contribute to the success of the enterprise. It is our plan to make this a popular movement, that this statue when erected, may be the New World's tribute to the noble Red Man who stood guard over the cradle in which its liberties were nurtured; and the principal object of the writer in preparing this compilation of historical facts has been to array these facts so that they will present a living, moving panorama of the long ago, an examination of which will disclose a complete justification of the enterprise in aid of which the book is written.

THE MEMORIAL

Fortunately, we have not been left in the dark concerning Massasoit's personal appearance. Edward Winslow, who was one of the hostages for his safe return when he entered the settlement at Plymouth to confer with Governor Carver, and who saw him on that occasion and often thereafter for many years, who was his friend, and one whom Massasoit loved, has left us such a complete and perfect description of him as is to be found of but few men of those remote times; and fortunately, we have succeeded in enlisting the services of Cyrus E. Dallin of Arlington, Massachusetts, eminent sculptor and portrayer of Indian character, to translate Winslow's description into bronze. Massasoit was forty-one years old when he first appeared to the Pilgrims, and Mr. Dallin has created a model of the proud warrior in the prime of life, bearing the peace pipe to the strangers from across the great waters. From this model it is proposed to erect a statue of heroic size to be appropriately mounted on

Cole's Hill, immediately overlooking the famous rock against which the Mayflower's shallop rested and upon which its occupants landed on December 21, 1620. The Pilgrim Society of Plymouth has offered the site, and has volunteered to assume perpetual care of the statue when erected. And so we present our case to the people of the United States in an appeal to them to participate in an enterprise, the purpose of which is to pay deserved but belated tribute to this great Chief, that he may forever stand guard over the gateway through which the pilgrim bearers of the torch of Liberty first entered New England, even as he kept a watchful eye over her early struggles for existence.

A. G. W.

FALL RIVER, MASS.
May 10, 1919.

CONTENTS

MASSASOIT OF THE WAMPANOAGS

MASSASOIT

I

INTRODUCTORY

ALMOST three hundred years have passed into history since the Pilgrim ship bearing its precious freight of human souls dropped anchor in Cape Cod Bay, and its occupants sent out their shallop in search of a suitable place for landing. English ships had visited the New England coast many times between the date of the discovery of the New World by Columbus and that day; but they had brought only explorers, adventurers, traders and fishermen. Unlike the long line of its predecessors, the *Mayflower* came laden with men, women and children, bringing with them all their earthly possessions; and, what was immeasurably more important, the Anglo-Saxon love of liberty, which, developed under the new conditions they found here, has given us the boon of perfect liberty and equality under the law, but not in contravention of law.

They had come to stay. Denied the right to worship God in such form and manner as they saw fit, persecuted for their non-conformity to the estab-

1

lished faith, they had fled from England to Holland, and from the latter country to the wilderness peopled only by natives who knew nothing of European civilization, European customs or European religion, beyond what little they had learned from traders; and that was not favorable to the Europeans.

The century preceding their coming had witnessed the most remarkable upheavals in the religious world of which history furnishes any record, except the advent of men who have promulgated an entirely new religion with such vigor that they have succeeded in impressing their teachings upon a considerable portion of the people of the world.

In 1517 Tetzel, a Dominican Friar, and the guardian of the Franciscan Friars had been appointed by the Cardinal Archbishop of Mainz, joint commissaries for Saxony and North Germany, to preach an indulgence to all who would contribute to the rebuilding of St. Peter's Church at Rome; and while Tetzel was preaching in the Schlosskirche at Juterbogk, Luther had nailed to the door of the kirche his ninety-five theses, in which he challenged Tetzel to a defence of his position, and took an attitude contrary to the established order, from which he ever after refused to recant.

A little later, Henry VIII of England, in consequence of a quarrel with the Pope and Cardinals concerning the dissolution of his marriage to Catherine of Aragon, had established the Church of England as an independent ecclesiastical body; and still later John Calvin, a Frenchman, born in the year that Henry ascended the throne of England, promulgated the Geneva Creed.

All these things had set the leaven of religious liberty into a ferment which nearly blew the lid off the mixing pan; and creeds without number sprang up, especially among people who had chafed under the restrictions which held them to forms of worship and to beliefs established by others, whom they thought no more capable of expounding the teachings of the founders of the religion they professed than were they. If Luther the priest could dissent from the teachings that had been inculcated into his mind through a long course of training for his profession; if the King of England, who had been a firm adherent of the established order of things, and had so ably defended the prerogatives of the church of Rome that he had been recognized by it as "Defender of the Faith," could set up an independent church, what limit was to be placed upon revolts against theological dogmas? What was to prevent the men who followed Luther, the English dissenters and Calvin in doing their own thinking, from doing a little independent thinking on their own account?

At any rate, this is just what happened, with the result that the dissenters from the dogma of the first dissenters found themselves in just as uncomfortable a position as that in which those first protestants against the established religion were placed by their protestations; for it is a peculiar characteristic of the human mind, that, having discovered what it considers error in the tenets of any faith, and set up its own standard, it at once becomes intolerant of any one who suggests or even thinks that he has the same right to dissent from the latest standard established. So we find the Church of England refusing to the followers of Calvin the same religious liberty they had claimed in their defiance of the Church of Rome.

It was this which drove the Pilgrims across the Atlantic in search of a home in the wilderness where they might be free from all restrictions upon their religious liberty; and by the irony of fate, it was this same working of the human mind, this same characteristic of which I have just spoken, that led them to acts of intolerance and oppression against men of other religious beliefs and the heterodox members of their own congregations, men whose consciences would not allow them to subscribe to all the tenets of the creed set up for them. It was this that drove Roger Williams from Salem to seek refuge first with Massasoit at Sowams, and later with the Narragansetts at the place which he devoutly named Providence; that sent Gorton from Plymouth to the same Narragansett country; and John Easton and a multitude of other Quakers from the Massachusetts Bay colony to Rhode Island and other places.

The Pilgrims and the Puritans came here in search of a home where they might be free, but closed their doors to others impelled by the same love of freedom to flee their native land, thus following the example of those whose persecutions they themselves had fled. In this they were but following the inscrutable workings of the human mind, and indirectly and unintentionally laying the foundations of a broader liberty than they ever beheld in their wildest flights of fancy; for the very intolerance which they displayed but sharpened the spirit of resistance, and led to a more thorough understanding of true liberty, the liberty to pursue one's own inclinations until the pursuit reaches the bounds of positive evil, or trespasses upon the like liberties of another.

These reflections are peculiarly applicable to the settlers of Southern New England, because they were the first to attempt to establish upon these shores the principle of religious liberty for themselves, though denied to others. The Roman Catholics in Maryland and the Quakers in Pennsylvania but followed the trail they blazed; and it is in consequence of these facts that we of New England claim for our barren soil the title of Birthplace of the American Ideal, which if carefully conserved and safeguarded, will become the ideal of the world. Our New England soil may not be as productive as that of the plains of our middle west or of our sunny south; but the atmosphere of New England civil and religious liberty that has surrounded us has been highly productive of men and women who have left the impress of their character upon the life of the country. In fact, I question whether any one will attempt at this late day to gainsay the claim so often made that December 21, 1620, was the natal day of the American system of government. Somewhat crude at its birth was the idea out of which that system has grown; but the intolerance of restraint in matters of thought was there, and it is this spirit of resistance to attempts to limit the freedom of thought and action, running through all our colonial history, that finally developed into that immortal document, the Declaration of Independence, written, it is true, by a lover of humanity from fair Virginia, but breathing in its every line the traditions of New England, which had ere that time become the traditions of an incipient nation.

The importance of that twenty-first day of December, 1620, and of the landing of the Pilgrim fathers at Plymouth as an event in the history of the country, aye of humanity, cannot be overestimated; nor can too high a valuation be put upon all the agencies that contributed to the success of the venture which drove them across the water. Foremost among those agencies was the attitude of the natives towards these invaders of their domain. Had they, in resentment of their treatment at the hands of white adventurers, explorers and traders, assumed a hostile attitude, with the limited means of making the long and dangerous voyage across the sea at that time, they could undoubtedly have wiped out the colonies as fast as they could have been planted, and thus set back the history of our country for at least a hundred years; the early history of New England would have been written in characters of blood on every hillside and plain instead of characters of living light for the illumination of the world; and without

the history of New England, the history of the
United States, aye, even of humanity, would be a
different tale from that we teach our children and
read in the record of current events.

The present moment, with the statesmen of the
free nations of the world assembled at Versailles
for the discussion of a means for securing the peace
of the world, seems a peculiarly appropriate time
for calling attention to the first peace conference
ever held on American soil, in which the white race
participated on equal terms with the aborigines, of
which we have any record; and its coming, as it
does, on the eve of the three hundredth anniversary
of that original conference, adds to the significance
of the treaty growing out of that conference.

It is not my purpose to write a history of the
early colonial days. Events as they occurred were
recorded by men who participated in them; and
later writers, whose name is legion, drawing their
information from these early historians, have dwelt
upon the facts they set down, with all the embel-
lishments capable of being given to them by the
thoughtful mind and the facile pen. He who attempts to write history three hundred years after
the happening of the events he records, with no
new facts, disclosed by research at sources hitherto
unexplored, must needs possess the skill to paint his
narrative in colors never before essayed, or content
himself with being a mere compiler of facts gathered
and recorded by others. Unless his is the faculty of
saying things in a more pleasing manner or of array-
ing his facts in such a way that they will present a

more attractive picture than has been before portrayed by them, his excuse for writing is indeed
small.

No new facts will be presented by the narrative
I am undertaking, nor do I lay claim to any magic
in the wielding of the pen that will make the old
appear new. All that I shall attempt is to rescue
from a mass of other matter in which they are so
buried as to be almost inaccessible to the reader
who has not the time or the inclination for wide
research, certain historic facts, with a view to calling
attention to some of the errors that have sprung up
concerning the aborigines whom our fathers found
in possession of this fair land when they first set
foot upon its shores; to array those facts, gleaned
from the writings of the men who participated in
the stirring events of which they write, in such
form that the array will assist in a better understanding and higher appreciation of the true relations between the original possessors of the land
and the invading settlers from the old world, than
the average reader is likely to gather from a limited
reading of early history in which the subjects to
which I desire to call attention are passed over
with a word.

Many of the most important features of that
early history are almost entirely lost to the majority
of readers for the reasons that I have suggested.
True, every reader of American history knows of
the struggles of the early settlers with hostile bands
of natives, and of their privations and hardships in
every form; he knows of the visit of Samoset to

the Pilgrims a few months after they landed at Plymouth and of his greeting, "Welcome, Englishmen"; he has heard something of Squanto and of Hobamock; but how much does he really know about them? And yet, the part played by them and others of their kind in the early struggles of the infant colony, their faithfulness to their treaty obligations and their loyalty and devotion to those to whom they had thereby bound themselves, form the brightest pages in the annals of Colonial New England.

The story of Canonicus of the Narragansetts, and his haughty challenge to the colonists at Plymouth, sent in the form of a bundle of arrows bound in a rattlesnake's skin, and of Governor Bradford's defiant reply, is familiar to every American schoolboy; but how many know that, following and probably in consequence of this incident, the Narragansetts were firm friends of the whites for more than twenty years, until the death of their beloved sachem Miantonomo, the nephew of Canonicus, at the hands of the fierce Uncas of the Mohicans? Probably every reader of American history remembers the story of that unjustifiable death, and of Uncas' cutting a slice of flesh from the shoulder of his still quivering victim and eating it, declaring it to be the sweetest meat he ever ate; but how many know that eight commissioners of the colonies in Massachusetts and Connecticut authorized this cold-blooded murder of one of the most faithful friends the whites had among the red men, and thereby aroused the hostility of the Narragansetts, the most powerful confederation in New England, to such an extent that it was never allayed until the extermination of that federation in King Philip's war?

Every one knows something about that war, but what percentage of even the well informed men of today can tell you any of the causes that led up to it, except possibly, the land question, which was really the least of the causes? How many know that Philip, the so-called "vindictive, bloodthirsty, cruel savage," showed more humanity in his treatment of whites during the war than was shown by the colonists towards their enemies?

Since writing the foregoing lines, my attention has been called to a matter which gives added force to what I have said concerning the general lack of information upon the subject of which I write. Within a few days the following appeared in a daily paper published in Providence.

"Miss Elizabeth B. Champlin, a direct descendant of the old Ninigret tribe of Indians which was so prominent in Southern Rhode Island more than a century ago, died at Westerly yesterday. She was 100 years and 10 months old, having been born just over the line in Connecticut on June 23, 1818.

"She was a resident of Westerly all her life practically, and was a daughter of Jesse and Hager Champlin, her father being a member of the Ninigret tribe."

I am not sufficiently familiar with the history of Rhode Island for the past hundred years to assert positively that there was not a tribe there known as the Ninigret Indians; but if a tribe under that name did exist, the appellation Ninigret was a misnomer, and probably was given to the remnant of the Niantic tribe which followed its sachem — Ninigret — in taking sides with the English in King Philip's war. The whites may have given them the name of their sachem after the war, meaning thereby simply Ninigret's Indians or Ninigret's tribe. The nearest approach to this name in the early histories is found in the records of one of the old writers who speaks of the Eastern Niantics as Ninnicrafts, this also being the name sometimes given to the sachem Ninigret; but Ninigret was a Niantic, and the Eastern Niantics being under the protection of the Narragansetts, and perhaps closely related to them, most early writers speak of him as one of the Narragansett sachems.

The news writer may be speaking from exact knowledge, but to the man interested in tracing names to their sources, the article referred to leaves too much to be further inquired into or simply inferred; and I call attention to the matter at this time solely for the purpose of emphasizing what I have said on the subject.

Wherever there is a lack of knowledge of many of these interesting facts, it is due simply to the tendency of the dominant race to exploit the deeds of its ancestors, and to a perfectly natural impulse on the part of the descendants of the empire builders of three centuries ago to dwell upon the courage, energy and devotion to principle of the sturdy men who braved the terrors of the deep and the dangers of an unknown land, to plant upon these shores a government founded upon ideals which they had developed.

And so, without attempting to write history or even to essay the work of a compiler, the writer has prepared the following brief sketches of character, groups, tribes, and men in such a way that a careful reading of the whole will present a living, moving panorama of the olden times, not a complete picture in any sense, but simply a sketch, a glimpse through the foliage that will reveal enough to lead to a better appreciation of the services rendered by the lost race in laying the foundations of our liberty. If my effort assists, in only a small degree, in securing a fair hearing before the tribunal of public opinion for a much maligned people, I shall feel that my labor has not been in vain. So bitter has been the arraignment of the red men by some of the writers of the early days, as well as by many who have followed them, that I have not hesitated to use language in characterizing their writings, and sometimes themselves, that may appear unnecessarily harsh; but there is such a perfectly apparent spirit of unfairness running through their narratives that they merit little sympathy.

One thing we cannot keep too constantly in mind, and that is that the red men left no records. The history of the events in which they participated was written, for the most part, by their enemies; and it is only by digging up a line here and a sentence there, that one is enabled to get together anything that will do justice to the character of the race they exterminated, and then, to justify their treatment of them, attempted, by their writings, to cover with infamy.

We can afford to approach the subject without passion or prejudice; and, reading between the lines, draw our own conclusions of the right and the wrong of the struggle for supremacy waged between the contending races. One is amazed to read from the pen of Schoolcraft, who wrote as late as 1849, such a sentiment as this concerning King Philip. "We may lament that such energies were misapplied, but we cannot withhold our respect for the man who, though lacking the motives that lead Christian martyrs to the stake and civilized heroes to the 'imminent deadly breach,' was yet capable of combining all the military strength and political wisdom of his country and placing the colonists in decidedly the greatest peril through which they had ever passed." This is the same Philip of whom Major Daniel Gookin, commander of the Middlesex regiment in the war, wrote, "he was a person of good understanding and knowledge of the best things," quoted with apparent approval by Schoolcraft.

Just what motives are referred to as leading "civilized heroes" to the "imminent deadly breach," that were lacking in Philip is not entirely clear, unless the author quoted means his readers to infer that what is a virtue in civilized heroes is a vice in those who are less civilized, or that the less civilized are devoid of sentiment and incapable of being moved by the law of self-preservation and the motive of defence of family, home and native land. "We may lament that such energies were misapplied." In fact, it is one of the things that ought to give us food for reflection and serious regret, that our fathers thought it necessary by their acts of oppression and wrong, to drive Philip and his followers to the misapplication of their energies, instead of turning them to the advantage of both races. We commend the "civilized heroes" of all ages and of all nations who have sprung to the "imminent deadly breach" in defence of all that life holds dear; and the same historians who sing their praises have illogically devoted their energies for more than two centuries to an attempt to palliate or excuse the crimes of the whites, by condemning the simple natives who remained steadfast in the defence of the same principles for which heroes have died since history began.

Speaking of King Philip's war in general, Schoolcraft continues: "It is interesting to observe the fate of this people who were the object of so much benevolent care after the passage of an epoch of little less than two centuries. The great blow to the permanent success of this work was struck by the unfortunate and general war which broke out under the indomitable sachem called Metacom, better known as King Philip. He drew all but the Christian converts and the Mohigans into this scheme. Even these were suspected. The cruelties which were committed during this war produced the most bitter hatred and distrust between the parties. The whole race of Indians was suspected and from the advance of this unwise war on

the part of the natives, we must date the suspicion
and unkind feelings which were so prevalent and
which yet take up the American mind."

"Benevolent care!" One knows not whether to
laugh in derision or to weep in pity at the utter lack
of discernment of the man who sees "benevolent
care" in systematic robbery and oppression, coupled
with wholesale degradation through the sale of rum.
This was the colonists' "benevolent care."

"The cruelties which were committed during this
war" were not confined to the period of the war.
They were begun by the English and systematically
carried out for thirty years before the natives saw
the doom of their people in their continuation and
rose in revolt; and during the war the balance is
on the wrong side of the ledger for the whites to
complain.

"The whole race of Indians was suspected," and
for a long time before, had been suspected of a desire to live in freedom; and "the suspicion and unkind feelings which were so prevalent and which yet
take up the American mind," have resulted from the
reading of the histories of prejudiced writers like
Hubbard, Mather, Schoolcraft and scores of others,
who, through prejudice, or a desire to cover the sins
of the fathers by raising such a storm of slander and
disparagement of the men whom they were bent to
destroy, as to becloud the vision, present only one
side of the case and appeal to their readers to pass
judgment on the merits of the whole cause from the
evidence thus adduced; or rather to accept their
judgment without looking at the other side.

Unfortunately for the memory of the vanished race, too many men are content to accept the dictum of such historians without question; but, on the other hand, fortunately for the cause of truth, the white man has, perhaps inadvertently, allowed enough to get into the records to enable the discerning and discriminating reader to reverse the judgment. The modern tendency to "hew to the line, let the chips fall where they may," is leading to a better understanding and a more favorable consideration of Indian character. A careful analysis of the history of the early colonies is bound to result in the shattering of many idols; but desperate indeed is the situation of any people whose past and present cannot stand the full glare of the searchlight of truth.

Our fathers have builded well, better perhaps than they dreamed; upon the foundations they laid, their sons have reared the superstructure of perfect liberty and equality before the law. Enough of credit and glory attaches to them, without attempting to cast a glamor of sanctity about them and their acts, to the discredit and infamy of the race they conquered and destroyed under a mistaken belief that its annihilation was necessary to make their own position secure.

This book is not written for savants. There is nothing in it that they do not know, although they may not agree with some of the writer's conclusions; but to the busy man who has not had the time or the inclination to make the little side trips into the realm of historical research that would enable him to discern what is true and what is false, we extend the invitation to come with us along the trails our fathers blazed, to go back in fancy over the ground they traversed, to take an account of the conditions they encountered; and to draw his own inferences and conclusions.

If the perusal of this series of little sketches presents nothing that has hitherto escaped your attention, let it, at least, refresh your recollection of the story of the olden times. Let it recall the hardships endured by the pioneers, the perils they faced to plant upon these new found shores the tree of liberty, and to nourish and sustain it in the early days of its growth, ere it had attained sufficient strength to withstand the blasts of adversity. Let it impress upon you the duty we owe to the memory of a vanished race to give it the full measure of credit to which it is entitled, as one of the agencies that contributed to the early growth and development of the colonies which gave us a nation. Without the friendship of that race, the history of New England would be written in different characters than it is today, and without New England, what would have been the history of America?

As we look back upon the past, comparing it as it was with what it might have been but for the friendship of Massasoit, and the beneficent effects of that friendship, as a bulwark of protection for that feeble band who laid the foundation of our free institutions, we shudder to think, "how weak a hand may turn the iron helm of fate"; by how slender a hair the sword of destiny hangs suspended above the heads of men and nations.

II

INDIAN CHARACTER

SO much has been said and written about the
character of the aborigines that the subject
may be thought to have been exhausted long ago;
and so it is, except as individual thought and individual analysis of the various appraisals of Indian
character may contribute to a better understanding
of it; for, notwithstanding the various estimates
that have been made, or rather in consequence of the
apparent contradictions in them, it may be worth
while to compare a few of them for the purpose of
ascertaining the cause of the contradictions, and determining whether there is any real conflict, or only
an apparent one resulting from the changes wrought
by time and circumstances. No value would attach
to such an attempt, but for the fact that we are too
prone to form our opinions from too limited reading,
in which we may see but one side of a matter; and
even if we have read both sides, the way in which
one writer has arrayed his facts, the language used,
in a word, the picture he presents, may make a more
lasting impression than that of any other, and so
we unconsciously form our opinion from that which
has thus appealed to us and written itself upon the
tablets of our memory most ineffaceably.

The principal difficulty with most of the later portrayals of Indian types and character that have been presented to us has been that they have painted the Indian as he was after generations of demoralizing contact with the white man and his civilization, demoralizing because first attempts to engraft civilization upon the natural stock inevitably result in the absorption by the children of nature of all the evils of civilization and the rejection of the good, just as children acquire evil habits more readily than correct ones, even when most zealously watched and guarded. The result of the early attempts to teach the aborigines of this continent the arts of civilization has been the creation of a character so immeasurably worse than that of the natives in their primitive state that one shudders to think of the monstrosity that grew out of the attempt. There is enough of evil in the best of men, and if only the good that has come to the advanced races, without its attendant evils, could be impressed upon the plastic minds of men in their natural state, thus leading them little by little away from the vices of barbarism without leading them into the vices of civilization, the history of the world would be written in different characters than it is. For no one will attempt to gainsay the fact that the enlightenment of ages has resulted, not only in the production of much that is of real value to the cause of progress and of humanity, but also of as much that has been a stumbling block to trip the unwary. Science has produced as much evil as good, and yet we would not descry science on that account, because the path is open before us to choose the good and reject the evil in so far as it affects our own most intimate life; so we would not destroy the good because it is accompanied by evil, but rather avoid, and assist those who grope in darkness to avoid, the pitfalls that science has dug for unwary feet. Had our fathers pursued this course, much that has been written concerning Indian character would not have found a place upon the pages of history.

Francis Parkman, Jr., from whose writings I shall have occasion to quote from time to time, although a man of painstaking research, and a vivid painter of word pictures, seems to have fallen into this general error of delineating the character of the red man as it was after he had fallen a victim to too many of the demoralizing vices introduced by contact with the white man's civilization, which have had a tendency to exaggerate many of the characteristics to which Parkman calls attention to such an extent that, in reading his description, we are constantly under the necessity of keeping this fact in mind and of using it as a pruning knife with which to lop off the artificial growths and reduce conditions he describes to their normal state.

His description, however, is so vivid and contains so much of truth as established by the incontrovertible facts disclosed by history, and such a remarkable commentary on the workings of the human mind, that I am taking the liberty of lifting it bodily from the introductory chapter of his story of the Conspiracy of Pontiac, making such comments as seem to me to be warranted; and asking the reader to consider it in the light of the facts to which I have called attention. He says:

"Of the Indian character much has been written foolishly, and credulously believed. By the rhapsodies of poets, the cant of sentimentalists, and the extravagance of some who should have known better, a counterfeit image has been tricked out, which might seek in vain for its likeness through every corner of the habitable earth; an image bearing no more resemblance to its original than the monarch of the tragedy and the hero of the epic poem bear to their living prototypes in the palace and the camp. The shadows of his wilderness home, and the darker mantle of his own inscrutable reserve, have made the Indian warrior a wonder and a mystery. Yet to the eye of rational observation, there is nothing unintelligible in him. He is full, it is true, of contradiction. He deems himself the centre of greatness and renown; his pride is proof against the fiercest torments of fire and steel; and yet the same man would beg for a dram of whiskey or pick up a crust of bread thrown to him like a dog from the tent door of a traveler. At one moment he is wary and cautious to the verge of cowardice; at the next he abandons himself to the very insanity of recklessness, and the habitual self-restraint which throws an impenetrable veil over emotion is joined to the wild, impetuous passions of a beast or a mad man. Such inconsistencies, strange as they seem in our eyes, when viewed under a novel aspect, are but the ordinary instincts of humanity. The qualities of the mind are not uniform in their action through all the relations of life. With different men and different races of men, pride, valor, prudence, have different forms of manifestation, and where in one instance, they lie dormant, in another they are keenly awake. The conjunction of greatness and littleness, meanness and pride, is older than the days of the patriarchs; and such antiquated phenomena, displayed under a new form in the unreflecting, undisciplined mind of a savage, call for no special wonder, but should rather be classed with the other enigmas of the fathomless heart."

I have been constrained to quote thus freely, because it illustrates what I have already said concerning the mongrel produced by crossing the native barbarism with the evils of civilization. Parkman has given us in some respects a perfect picture of the child of the forest; but in parts of his characterization he has portrayed him as he was after he had been robbed of his lands, driven from his hunting grounds, defrauded of his petty substance and reduced to starvation by the ruthless destroyers of his race; his savage nature rendered a thousand times more savage by the white man's outrages and the white man's rum. Before contact with the white race had reduced him to the condition described by Parkman in some of these passages, Gosnold, Rofier and Smith met him, and their testimony establishes his character in his original state.

Continuing Parkman says: — "Some races of men seem moulded in wax, soft and melting, at once plastic and feeble. Some races, like some metals, combine the greatest flexibility with the greatest strength. But the Indian is hewn out of rock. You cannot change the form without destroying the substance. He will not learn the arts of civilization and he and his forest must perish together." This was written in 1851, and the last sentence has since been so completely refuted by the experience of the past quarter century that it almost leads us to doubt the accuracy of the entire appraisal. Some parts of it however, so perfectly accord with what we have learned from other sources that we may safely accept the whole, making due allowance for what are simply conclusions, and for the demoralizing effects of the agencies to which I have already called attention.

In conclusion Parkman says, "He has a hand bountiful to bestow as it is rapacious to seize, and even in extremest famine, imparting its last morsel to a fellow sufferer, a heart which, strong in friendship as in hate, thinks it not too much to lay down life for its chosen comrade; a soul true to its own idea of honor, and burning with an unquenchable thirst for greatness and renown." All of which leads us back to his reflection that these are "but the ordinary instincts of humanity," and "should be classed with the other enigmas of the fathomless heart."

Far out on the western plains or in the foot hills of the Rocky Mountains during the life and death struggle between the ever receding wave of red men and the restless ever advancing wave of invading whites, originated a saying which has been so often repeated that most of us have come to accept it as a truism, without stopping to consider all the facts that have contributed to the condition which gave rise to the expression. "There is no good Indian but a dead Indian," said some one of the men who had been sent either to quell some uprising among the natives, or to remove them from the lands their fathers had hunted and fished for generations, or that had been allotted to them at some earlier period when the cupidity of the whites, coveting their former abode, even as they now coveted the later, impelled them to press the red skins farther and farther towards the setting sun. Error, oft repeated, sometimes assumes the appearance of truth, and acts of cruelty often lent color to the maxim. Before accepting this judgment as final, however, it will be well to look into the characteristics of the race; compare them with other races that have not attained the topmost round of the ladder of civilization and consider the treatment accorded them by the whites. In this way, and only in this way, will we be able to determine whether the author of the expression has made an accurate appraisal of the Indian character. If we look upon the Indian as a child, and regard that child as a good child or otherwise in proportion to his promptness in doing as he is told, it will be difficult to deny the truth of the saying. If by good Indian, we mean the Indian who is willing to submit to every indignity and insult that the ingenuity of civilization can devise, who will permit himself to be kicked from pillar to post without protesting

in the most forcible manner known to him, who is
willing to give up to others the lands of his fathers,
who kisses the hand that smites him, and grovels
in the dust before the people who would rob him
and reduce him to virtual slavery, it is useless to
attempt to gainsay the maxim; and, by the same
standard, there is no good man, whether his skin
be red, or white, black, brown or yellow, but a dead
man, for a careful study of history inevitably leads
to the conclusion that human nature is very much
the same regardless of the color of a man's skin;
and that any man with red blood in his veins will
fight with such weapons as he possesses, and according to his light, for much the same ideals, foremost
among which is the protection of his home and
family and the graves of his fathers, for

"How can man die better than facing fearful odds
  For the ashes of his fathers and the temples of his gods,
  And for the tender mother that dawdled him to rest,
  And the gentle wife that fondles his children to her
    breast ? "

To form a correct estimate of Indian character,
it will be necessary to look into their life before it
had been influenced by contact with the whites, and
to inquire how their life and character have been
affected by that contact.

Every student of American history knows of the
reception of Columbus by the untutored children of
the islands, and of the homage they paid to the
wonderful strangers who had come from the land of
the rising sun in great canoes with the wings of a
bird; of the courtesy and kindness of the natives

to them, the treasures they freely bestowed upon them; and of the way in which the whites repaid their courtesy and kindness, by seizing their people and carrying them unwilling captives to Spain. This same kindness and courtesy were extended to nearly all the early explorers, and repaid in nearly all instances in the same way. Following the example of Columbus, and the early Spanish explorers, John and Sebastian Cabot in 1497 seized and carried away three natives to be exhibited as curiosities at the court of Henry VII. Caspar Cortereal, a Portuguese navigator, in 1500 captured a number and sold them into slavery. These are only two concrete examples of what was undoubtedly the general practice among the adventurers who crossed the ocean in those early days in search of the treasures of the Indies. In spite of this, Bartholomew Gosnold in 1602, after more than a century of such outrages, says of them, "These people are exceeding courteous, gentle of disposition, and well conditioned." In 1605, Sir Ferdinando Gorges, who was at that time the commander of the Port of Plymouth, England, sent Captain George Waymouth to the New England coast on a trading expedition. There is some disagreement among historians as to the exact place of the episode of which James Rofier, a member of his crew, and apparently the official secretary of the expedition, wrote, some placing it in the Narragansett country and others at Pemaquid on the Maine coast. Rofier writes, "When we came on shore, they most kindly entertained us, taking us by the hand and brought us to

sit down by their fire; they filled their pipes and
gave us of their excellent tobacco as much as we
would." This kind entertainment was repaid as related by Rofier in a communication dated June 14,
1605. "About eight o'clock this day, we went on
shore with our boats to fetch aboard water and wood.
Our captain, leaving word with the gunner in the
ship, by discharging a musket, to give notice if they
espied any canoe coming and which they did about
ten o'clock. He therefore, being careful they should
be kindly treated, requested me to go aboard, intending with dispatch to make what haste after he
possibly could. When I came to the ship, there
were two canoes and in either of them three savages,
of whom two were below at the fire; the others
seated in their canoes about the ship, and because
we could not entice them aboard, we gave them a
can of peas and bread, which they carried to the
shore to eat; but one of them brought back our can
presently and staid aboard with the other two; for
he being young of a ready capacity, and one we
most desired to bring with us into England had
received exceeding kind usage at our hands and was
therefore much delighted in our company. When
our captain was come, we consulted how to catch
the other three at shore, which we performed thus:
we manned the Lighthorseman [boat] with seven or
eight men; one, standing before, carried our box of
merchandise as we were wont when I went to
traffic with them, and a platter of peas, which meat
they loved, but before we were landed one of them
(being so suspiciously fearful of his own good) with-

drew himself into the wood. The other two met us on the shore side to receive the peas, with which we went up the cliff to their fire and sat down with them; and while we were discussing how to catch the third man who was gone, I opened the box and showed them trifles to exchange, thinking thereby to have banished fear from the other, and drawn him to return; but when we could not, we used little delay but suddenly laid hands upon them and it was as much as five or six of us could do to get them into the Lighthorseman; for they were strong, and so naked as our best hold was by their long hair on their heads; and we would have been very loth to have done them any hurt, which of necessity we had been constrained to have done if we had attempted them in a multitude; which we must and would rather than have wanted them, being a matter of great importance for the full accomplishment of our voyage."

Among these five was Tahanedo, a Sagamore. Sir Ferdinando Gorges writes of them that when they landed at Plymouth, England, he seized them and, further, that they were all of one nation but of several parts and several families, and concludes, "This accident must be acknowledged the means, under God, of putting on foot and giving life to all our plantations; and having kept them fully three years, I made them able to set me down what great rivers run up into the land, what men of note were seated on them, of what power they were, how allied, and what enemies they had."

The reason given for this kidnapping of the

natives by Waymouth was, not for the purpose of making slaves of them, but to treat them kindly and thus induce them to give his employers information concerning the country that could not otherwise be obtained — a fine distinction in the view of our modern ideas of slavery. They were to be held for a long period of time against their will, to perform service for the men by whom they were held, but not as slaves.

It appears that in 1606, two of these captives were sent out with Captain Henry Challons on a trading expedition, but Challons and the natives were captured by the Spaniards. How long they were held does not appear, but they are both known to have returned to England at a later date.

In 1611, another of Gorges' captains, Edward Harlow, seized three natives at "Monhigon" Island. One of them got away and, gathering a number of others with him, he made a demonstration against the ship and cut loose a boat which they took to the shore, and which the ship's crew were unable to retake. Harlow then went south as far as "Capoge" (undoubtedly Martha's Vineyard). My reason for saying undoubtedly Martha's Vineyard is the similarity between this name and one of the Indian names of that island, Capawack, and the further fact that the name of one of the men whom he seized there is identical with that of the sachem of that island in 1621. At Capoge, Harlow seized two Indians named Coneconam and Epenow, and at Nohono, he seized another named Sakaweston. With these five he returned to England.

In 1614 still another of Gorges' captains named Hobson, on an expedition to the New England coast brought back Epenow with him. It is related that when he arrived in his native country, Epenow conspired with some of his friends to effect his escape, and that they came to rescue him with twenty canoes; that Epenow slipped from the ship, and his friends in the canoes let fly such a shower of arrows upon and about the ship that its crew were unable to retake him.

In 1619, Captain Thomas Dermer, another of Gorges' captains, on the occasion of his visit to the New England coast, met Epenow, who told him of his escape. Epenow learned from him that he was in Gorges' service and made inquiry about him, but probably believing that Dermer had been sent to recapture him and take him back to England, he gathered a number of his people and attacked Dermer, apparently with the intent to take him prisoner; "but he being a brave stout gentleman," drew his sword and freed himself from them, though not without much difficulty, as it is related that he received fourteen wounds in the encounter, of so serious a nature that he was obliged to go to Virginia to have them attended to.

It was on the occasion of this visit that Dermer learned of another outrage perpetrated by the whites upon the natives. In a letter dated June 20, 1620, he writes that the Pokanokets "bear an inveterate malice to the English"; and that this enmity was "aroused by an Englishman, who had many of them on board, and made a great slaughter with their murderers [small cannon or mortars] and small shot, when, as they say, they offered no injury." Dermer doubts whether these were English or French, who, as Winslow learned on the occasion of his visit to Sowams in 1621, did much fishing in Narragansett Bay. Whether English or French is not of much consequence. They were whites, and their act would naturally arouse the ire of the outraged natives against the white race. From our knowledge of the treatment of the natives by the French as compared with that of the English, however, we are safe in concluding that Dermer had very little reason for the doubt. This was another chapter in the history of malicious treatment of the Indians which would never have seen the light of day but for this letter of Captain Dermer.

In this connection, the fact that this attack was made upon the people of the same Great Sachem who less than a year after the letter was written and probably within seven or eight years of the time of the outrage of which Dermer writes, trailed forty miles to Plymouth to extend to the Pilgrims the olive branch of peace, is worth a word of comment in passing.

In 1614 Captain John Smith with a fleet of trading vessels visited the new world and skirted the shores of New England from the Penobscot to and around Cape Cod. From his observations made on this occasion, he drafted a map of the coast, a copy of which appears in Governor William Bradford's history of Plymouth Colony, as published by the Massachusetts Historical Society. This map,

though not without its inaccuracies, shows such
familiarity with the coast that it inevitably leads to
the conclusion that Smith must have made a careful
study of the topography of the shore; and there
can be no doubt that he made very many landings
all along this coast. If this is true, what he says
concerning Indian traits must be taken as applying
generally, and not to any particular tribe or to those
of any special locality. Captain Smith, writing of
the natives at that time, says "they were silly
savages," and "they were very kind, but in their
fury no less valiant, for upon a quarrel we had with
one of them, he only with three others, crossed the
harbor of Quonahassit [Cohasset] to certain rocks
whereby we had to pass, and there let fly their
arrows for our shot." As Smith proceeded down
the bay "upon small occasion," as he writes, further
difficulty arose, some forty or fifty Indians attacking
the English. The exact place of this encounter is
not given, but it was either in the territory of the
Massachusetts or that of the Wampanoags. It is
recorded that on this occasion the English fired upon
the natives, killing one and wounding another with
a shot through the thigh; and yet we are told on no
less an authority than that of Smith himself, that in
an hour after the encounter, they made up and were
friends again. It was on this voyage that Captain
Smith, sailing from the coast of New England for
Virginia, left one of his vessels, under command of
Captain Thomas Hunt, in Cape Cod Bay, to complete the loading of his ship with fish, furs and oil.
Captain Hunt, relieved of the restraint of his su-

perior, completed his cargo, and then to his eternal infamy, enticed twenty-seven natives on board, and sailed away with them to Malaga where he sold them into slavery. These twenty-seven were made up of twenty Patuxets and seven Nausets, among the former of whom was Squanto, about whom we shall see more hereafter, as well as of the fate of the others.

The purpose of introducing these narratives briefly in this place has been to throw such light as they afford upon the character of the aborigines as they were first seen by the bold explorers and traders from Europe. I have quoted freely from the writings of the men who mingled with them after the acts of violence to which I have called attention, some of which occurred in the immediate vicinity of the Indians whose kindly traits were so clearly manifested, or in such close proximity to them that knowledge of the outrages on the part of the English must have reached the men who still received them with open arms, and appeared desirous of maintaining friendly relations with them, and of bartering their valuable furs for such trinkets and baubles as appealed to their native simplicity. The testimony of all these men is to the same effect, and establishes beyond peradventure the fact that they were kind, courteous, hospitable and of gentle disposition. "Silly savages" they may have been, in the sense that they knew not the value of what they gave, measured by the standard of what their received, unskilled in the arts of commerce, but not the treacherous and blood-thirsty fiends that their descendants have been painted; not entirely without cause it must be admitted, but, what is the cause?

It is undoubtedly true that training for war was looked upon as the most important part of the education of the Indian youth, and that wars between the tribes were waged altogether too frequently and without what would be considered justifiable cause among civilized peoples; and no attempt has ever been made to controvert the charge so often made that unnecessary cruelties were indulged in by the warring nations. I shall not attempt to justify burning prisoners at the stake or the practice of removing a portion of a war victim's scalp as a trophy of the conflict; but will content myself by simply calling attention to the fact that all human progress has been by slow stages and that, as nations have climbed the ladder of civilization round by round, they have, with each successive upward movement, shaken off some of the practices of the lower life in which their fathers had indulged; but that this climbing has been going on through countless ages, and that the conduct of each succeeding generation has been according to its light. Old customs die hard, and it is much easier to walk in the trodden path than to blaze new trails. The primitive red men who occupied the land at the time of its discovery by Europeans had made comparatively little progress along the path of civilization, though they were not the totally benighted children of evil that some would have us believe. They still lived, for the most part, by hunting and fishing, and the num-

ber of people who can subsist in this way upon any
given territory is necessarily limited by the natural
increase in the game and fish. They had no domes-
tic animals, and for meat depended upon the hunt.
They were, therefore, extremely zealous in guarding
the boundaries of their hunting grounds to protect
them against trepasses by the occupants of neighboring localities; and any serious invasion of their
territory which resulted in the taking of the game
which meant life or death to them was a most serious offence, and one that was almost certain to result in war. And these wars were frequently waged
to the complete extermination or subjugation of one
of the contending parties. This was not necessarily
the result of any inherent cruelty or love of killing
one's enemies merely for the sake of killing, but for
the purpose of so reducing them as to make further
acts of violence either to the persons of the conquerors or against their hunting grounds a matter
of the remotest possible chance; as well as to make
of them an example that would strike terror into the
hearts of other possible trespassers. They had not
made the progress that enabled them to discard, in
their treatment of their slain or captured enemies,
the practices they had learned from their fathers;
although there is no doubt that they had ameliorated
the conditions of warfare to some considerable extent since the beginning of their history. They
simply lived according to the light the Great Spirit
had vouchsafed them, and, if left to themselves,
might, by the long and tedious process of racial
evolution, have developed a civilization which would

compare favorably with that of the nations of the old world. It has been said of them that they never forgave an injury or forgot a benefit. Too many of their critics, in considering their character, forget the last part of this saying. But, taking the testimony of the men who mingled freely with them as establishing the characteristics to which I have alluded, how shall we account for the atrocities perpetrated upon the whites by the sons of the men whom Gosnold, Rofier and Smith describe? Perhaps the first intimation of one great cause is to be found in Governor Bradford's account of the entertainment of Samoset at Plymouth on the sixteenth and seventeenth of March, 1621. Samoset came from Monhegan, the island from which Harlow carried away two natives in 1611, and probably in close proximity to the place of Captain Waymouth's adventure a few years before. Monhegan was one of the noted Indian fishing places and was frequently resorted to by English visitors to these parts before and after the times referred to. It was in fact the site of one of the earliest English attempts at colonization in New England. Samoset had mingled with the English voyagers sufficiently to pick up a few words of their language and apparently had acquired a taste for English beer, for Bradford tells us that he asked for that beverage on the occasion of his first entertainment at Plymouth, and was given "strong water." Ah! There is one answer to the degradation of the "silly savages." "Strong water." The Indian's "fire water," first supplied to them by the whites, whether for the purpose of so benumbing their senses that they would lose what little cunning they had in trading or of creating an appetite so insatiable that they would barter the fruits of the hunt for an exhilarating draught of the beverage, we can only conjecture, but we have seen so much of its effects upon man that it is not difficult to hazard an inference concerning the result. We have seen men spend the price of their children's food to obtain it; we have seen the mother under its influence desert her offspring; the son curse the mother that gave him birth; and raise his hand against the father who guided his first tottering steps in infancy. We have seen it transform the mild and kindly disposition into the fury of a demon; and it is not difficult for us to picture the change that would be wrought in the simple natives, the "silly savages," by its insidious influence. Add to this the treatment they received at the hands of the whites, and the story is complete. Their hospitality and kindness repaid by violence, captivity and slavery; their hunting grounds given over to the axe and the plow; their means of securing a livelihood constantly diminished by these encroachments upon the lands they had inherited from their fathers. What more is needed to efface whatever progress a thousand years had seen, to arouse and intensify all the old savage instincts that more careful consideration and kindly treatment might have obliterated? Instead of taking careful account of the slumbering demon within them and repaying kindness with kindness, the whites hurled among them the firebrand of robbery, causeless slaughter,

slavery and outrage; and, because the wrongs of a
hundred years coupled with the white man's rum
transformed the "silly savage," kind, courteous
and hospitable, into the blood-thirsty red skin of the
period beginning with the death of Miantonomo and
terminating only with the complete subjugation of
the race on the western plains and in the mountain
fastnesses of the Cordilleras, we are told that
"There is no good Indian but a dead Indian."

The red man has been called blood-thirsty, cruel,
vindictive, false and treacherous, these being pronounced by some writers the predominating traits
of the character of the race.   There is much in their
dealings with each other and with the whites to sub-
stantiate the charge; but before passing judgment
on his race, let us look at him in comparison with
the men against whom he stood for the defence of
his native land; and then "let him that is without
sin first cast a stone." Let torture stand as the
test of cruelty; and, in torture, the Mohican allies
of the Colonists were the past masters among the
New England Indians. Take the most cruel case
recorded in history to establish the charge, the case
related by an early historian.   Among the prisoners
captured by Major Talcott of Connecticut was a
young Narragansett, who had been taken by some
of the Mohicans; and they asked permission to put
him to death by torture. Hubbard tells us this
was exceedingly painful for the English, and then
proceeds to say that one of the reasons for granting
the permission was "that they might have an ocular
demonstration of the savage, barbarous cruelties of

these heathen"; who, by the way, were their allies, and whose cruelties they sanctioned, knowing them to be the most cruel and savage of the natives. The other reason for granting the permission was, "lest by a denial they might disoblige their Indian friends." Now read Hubbard's description of what occurred.

"The Narragansett boasted that he had killed nineteen Englishmen and had loaded his gun for the twentieth, but not finding one, he had shot a Mohegan rather than lose a good shot." His tormentors "made a great circle and placed him in the middle so that all eyes might at the same time be pleased with the utmost revenge upon him. They first cut one of his fingers round in the joint at the trunck of the hand with a sharp knife and then brake it off; then they cut off another and another until they had dismembered one hand of all its digits, the blood sometimes spurting out in streams a yard from his hands, which barbarous unheard of cruelties, the English were not able to bear, it forcing tears from their eyes. Yet did not the sufferer ever relent or show any sign of anguish, for being asked by some of his tormentors how he liked the war, this insensible and hard-hearted monster answered he liked it very well and found it as sweet as Englishmen did their sugar. In this frame he continued until his executioners had dealt with the toes of his feet as they had done with the fingers of his hands, all the while making himself dance around the circle and sing, until he wearied both himself and them. At last they brake the bones of

his legs, for which he was forced to sat down, which
it is said he silently did, till they had knocked out
his brains."

For the highest refinement in cruelty commend
me to this, permitted, countenanced, encouraged
and witnessed by the whites, professed followers of
Him who walked in Galilee, teaching peace and
good will to men. Cruel on the part of the Mohicans! Certainly! Humane on the part of the
English? There was not a Wampanoag, a Narragansett or a Nipmuck fighting under Metacomet,
who would not have dashed into the circle and
despatched the sufferer with one blow of the tomahawk before the completion of this orgy of cruelty;
yet the Christian English saw it through. Search
the annals of that war as written by white men, and
you will search in vain for such an atrocity on the
part of their enemies.

Indiscriminate slaughter is evidence of blood-
thirstiness, and the entire history of the war is a
history of indiscriminate slaughter. It was a war
of extermination. Settlements were destroyed, men,
women and children sharing the same fate. At
Kingston, Rhode Island, during the swamp fight,
the whites set fire to every habitable hut or tepee
and burned hundreds of women and children.

When Awashonk, the squaw sachem of the Sa-
konnets, and her devoted band were surrounded,
the entire remnant of the tribe numbering ninety-
six were killed. When Tuspaquin, the "Black
Sachem" of Assawamsett, gave himself up on the
promise of a captaincy under Church, the first thing

that was done was to confront him with a firing squad to see if he was bullet proof, the pretense being that this was the condition on which the promise depended — a condition undoubtedly added after he had surrendered, for no one ever accused Tuspaquin of being so devoid of reason as to voluntarily give himself up on a promise with such a string as that attached to it.

They were vindictive, in the words of the men who exposed the head of Weetamo, the squaw sachem of Pocasset, on a pole at Taunton; who divided with the Mohicans, Niantics and Pequots the "glory of destroying so great a prince" as Canonchet, one shooting him, another cutting off his head and quartering his body and another burning the quarters. They were vindictive according to the testimony of the men who exposed the head of Philip on a pole at Plymouth for more than twenty years, after quartering his body and hanging the quarters in the trees where he fell; and who sold his wife and child (the grandson of Massasoit) into slavery with thousands of other captives.

They were false and treacherous, say the men who again and again promised amnesty to such as would come in and give themselves up, and, when they came in by hundreds, shot the leaders and sold the others into slavery. Compare this with Awashonk's conduct when Captain Church came to treat with her and found himself surrounded by her warriors. She had made no promises, and yet he came to confer, and she would not allow him to be injured.

Search the white man's record of the entire war

and you will grow weary in searching before you will find three instances of common decency on the part of the whites to parallel the three I am about to relate.

When the Indians approached Providence in 1676, Roger Williams went out alone to meet them to try to dissuade them from their purpose of attacking the town. He was seventy-seven years of age. "Massachusetts," said he, "can raise thousands of men at this moment, and if you kill them, the king of England will supply their places as fast as they fall." "Let them come," replied the savages, "we are ready. But as for you, Brother Williams, you are a good man. You have been kind to us many years. Not a hair of your head shall be touched." And they kept their promise.

At the commencement of hostilities at Swansea, the Indians captured two young sons of Sergeant Hugh Cole and carried them to their camp. King Philip, on hearing of this, ordered that no harm should be done them, and sent a guard to shield them from danger till they should arrive home; for as this "cruel, bloodthirsty, vindictive, false and treacherous" savage said, "their father sometime showed me kindness." King Philip, on the return of the boys, sent word to Sergeant Cole that it would be better to remove his family from Swansea, as it might not be in his power to prevent the Indians from doing them injury. Cole took his advice and removed his family to the island of Rhode Island; and they were not out of sight of their house when it was fired by the Indians.

There was a man named James Brown living in Swansea who was under the special protection of King Philip, who ordered his people to do no harm to him, because, as he said, his father (Massasoit) in his life time, had charged him to show kindness to Mr. Brown.

Find an instance in all the history of that war which shows a Colonist manifesting any gratitude for kindnesses if you can; point out a case where one of them refrained from staining his hands with the blood of Indian men, women and children, because a parent, fifteen years or more before, had requested that kindness be shown; and you will show a man competent to pass judgment on the Indians.

Place their records in parallel columns, and compare them carefully, with nothing to indicate which is the white man's record and which is the Indian's, and you will have difficulty in determining, with the chances strongly in favor of your making a mistake; consider them as they stand, knowing which is the white man's and which the Indian's, and you will find no difficulty in concluding that the terms civilized Christian and savage pagan are reversed; and that, as shown by their records, they should be savage Christian and civilized pagan.

The Indian "never forgave an injury, nor forgot a benefit." The latter part of this saying is proven true by the three historical anecdotes I have just related. The white man, of that period, never forgave an injury or remembered a benefit, except as ground for demanding another. And these are the men from whom we secure the information upon which we are to pass judgment on the Indian character; or rather whose estimate of that character we are asked to accept as final and conclusive. Fortunately for the memory of the lost race, their enemies have left enough behind in their records to enable men who look at those records without passion or prejudice to reverse the judgment.

III

THE ALGONQUINS

AMERICA, at the time of its discovery by Europeans, was peopled by a race whose origin has ever remained a matter of conjecture; whence they came and their relationship, if any, to other peoples who then occupied or had occupied other portions of the known world has remained one of the unsolved problems of the race; nor is it of any particular interest except as an abstract question of ethnology whether they were the descendents of the lost tribes of Israel or of the Hyksos, or Shepherd Kings of Egypt, or of the Tyrians, each of which had played its part in the drama of life and disappeared from the stage. Whether they had in some remote period crossed from the Eastern hemisphere, or were indigenous to the soil are problems that arouse the interest of the student of sociology, because they raise the question whether the Indians of the fifteenth and sixteenth centuries had relapsed into a state of at least semi-barbarism from the civilization of Europe, Asia and Northern Africa as developed centuries before, or had advanced by slow stages from the more complete barbarism of primitive men.

For the purpose of this work, we will take them as they were, leaving the problem of their origin and development to be discussed, or further discussed, by scientists in the hope that, as matter of abstract knowledge, the wisdom of future ages may penetrate the veil. Taking them as the Europeans found them, ethnologists tell us that the territory now included within the bounds of the United States, excluding Alaska and the islands of the seas, was occupied by seven distinct families, three of which, the Algonquin, Iroquois and Appalachian, sometimes called the Mobilian, were east of the Mississippi River.

As our interest at this time is limited to those tribes located in Southern New England, I shall not make further reference to the latter group which lay south of the Carolinas, nor to the Iroquois except to call attention to their activities, as those activities affected the Algonquin tribes located along the shores of the rivers, lakes and sea and in the forest fastnesses of New England.

Of the Iroquois, or Hodenosaunee, as they called themselves, the Five Nations of New York were the dominant league, and eventually, being joined by a sixth, thus making them the six nations, as they are frequently called, they overcame and absorbed the other tribes of their own race; and so in later times the six nations and Iroquois became almost identical in meaning. The original five nations were the Mohawks, Oneidas, Onondagas, Cayugas and Senecas. The Tuscaroras had at some earlier time broken away and settled on the coast and streams of the Carolinas, where they maintained themselves against the hostile attacks of Algonquins and Appalachians for generations, but were eventually reunited with their ancient brethren. The subjugated Iroquois tribes, the remnants of which were absorbed by the five nations, were the Hurons or Wyandots, Eries and Andastes. Whence they came, to have thus settled themselves in the limited territory they occupied, entirely surrounded by Algonquins, is uncertain. They themselves have three traditions concerning the matter, one of which tells us that they came from the north, another that they came from the west, and the third that they sprang from the soil of New York State.

The totemic clan seems to have been more highly developed among them than among the Algonquins, the several tribes, independently of their tribal relations, being united in eight such clans, the members of which were bound together by ties stronger than those of tribal relationship, intermarriage between members of the same clan being prohibited, though allowed between members of the same tribe but of different clans.

Francis Parkman, Jr., than whom no historian has taken greater pains to secure absolute accuracy, says of them: "They extended their conquests and their depradations from Quebec to the Carolinas, and from the Western prairies to the forests of Maine. On the South they forced tribute from the subjugated Delawares and pierced the mountain fastnesses of the Cherokees with incessant forays. On the North they uprooted the ancient settlement of the Wyandots, on the West they exterminated the Eries and the Andastes, and spread havoc and dismay around the tribes of the Illinois; and on the East the Indians of New England fled at the first peal of the Mohawk War Cry. Their war parties roamed over half America, and their name was a terror from the Atlantic to the Mississippi; but when we ask the numerical strength of the dreaded confederacy, when we discover that, in the days of their greatest triumphs, their united cantons could not have mustered four thousand warriors, we stand amazed at the folly and dissension which left so vast a region the prey of a handful of bold marauders.''

From this it is readily seen that they were a warlike people, dreaded by the Algonquins everywhere, by whom they seem to be known simply as Mohawks, this being perhaps the dominant tribe in the league. The period of their greatest triumph appears to have been from 1649 to 1672, for it was then that they subjugated their own kindred tribes, the Hurons, Eries and Andastes, and overran the Delawares.

One of the peculiar customs of the Iroquois is worth a word in passing, and that is the rule of descent through the female line; that is, a chief's brother, sister or sister's children succeeded to the chieftaincy rather than his own or his brother's children, the reason being that by no inconstancy on the part of the wife of a chief or of his mother or sisters, was it possible that his brother, sister or sister's children should not be of his own family, even if only through the mother, while the children of his wife or of his brother's wife might be no relation to him.

Such were the neighbors on the west of the Indians of New England in whom we are more particularly interested in connection with this work, but whose history is such a mixture of wars among themselves resulting from what appear to be successive waves of migration, constantly driven down to the New England coast through their inability to plant their feet on the lands preëmpted by the Iroquois; and wars with the Mohawks themselves, who crowded them so close on the west that no sketch of the eastern Algonquins is quite complete without considering briefly these neighbors who had succeeded in some way in planting themselves upon or within the Algonquin territory, where they remained, a pestilential thorn in the flesh of the tribes surrounding them.

Of the three eastern groups or families, the Algonquins were undoubtedly the most numerous and extended over the largest expanse of territory. Their dominion, excepting the region south of Lakes Erie and Ontario, and the peninsula between these lakes and Lake Huron, which was occupied by the Iroquois, extended from Hudson's Bay to the Carolinas and from the Atlantic to the Mississippi and Lake Winnipeg. To quote again from Parkman: "They were Algonquins who greeted Jacques Cartier, as his ships ascended the St. Lawrence. The first British Colonists found savages of the same race hunting and fishing along the coasts and inlets of

Virginia, and it was the daughter of an Algonquin chief who interceded with her father for the life of the adventuresome Englishman. They were Algonquins, who, under Sassacus the Pequot and Philip of Mt. Hope, waged deadly war against the Puritans of New England, who dwelt at Pennacook under the rule of the great magician, Passaconaway, and trembled before the evil spirits of the Crystal Hills; and who sang *Aves* and told their beads in the forest chapel of Father Rasles, by the banks of the Kennebec. They were Algonquins, who under the great tree at Kensington, made the covenant of peace with William Penn."

In the year 1000 when Thorvald with his viking crew sought to establish a colony at Vinland, this group of the American Indians was limited to much narrower confines. The skroellings whom he encountered and at whose hands he met his fate, during the five centuries that elapsed between his adventurous attempt and the next recorded visits of Europeans, had been driven north by advancing waves of Algonquin migration; and their descendants are still occupying the frozen regions of the far north. Esquimau, we call them, signifying in the Algonquin tongue, "Eaters of Raw Fish." What took place during those five centuries is matter of conjecture; but there are certain historical facts that make it possible to draw inferences supported by reason.

The Leni Lenapee, in their own tongue, the Loups of the French, the Delawares of the English, call themselves the parent stock of the Algonquin group, and their claim seems to be admitted by the other branches. The name by which they designate themselves means "original men," and in speaking of or to the members of other tribes of the family, they used the terms, little brothers, children, grandchildren or nephews, and the other tribes referred to them as father or grandfather.

So it is likely that the Algonquin group had its origin, or at some remote time had established itself, in the vicinity of New Jersey, Delaware, Maryland and eastern Pennsylvania, and as its original limits became too narrow it spread out to the North, the East, the South and the West in successive waves of migration, each driving the preceding one further and further away from the home of its fathers.

Schoolcraft believes that the Wolf Totem, or Mohicans, were the first of the three clans of the Lenapee to migrate, locating near Albany, whence they were driven over the Hoosic and Pekonet ranges into the valley of the Housatonic; and Gallatin says this was the only one of the subdivisions to leave their ancient hunting grounds. Neither expresses any opinion whether they were forced eastward from the Hudson by other migratory bands of Algonquins from the parent stock or by the Iroquois; and there appears to be nothing in the works of early historians that furnishes any evidence, gathered by men who have made a study of Indian lore and traditions at their sources, whether the Iroquois were there before the Algonquins in such strength that they could not be forced back, but allowed the latter to sweep around them, or came down from the west or north and met the advancing movement of the Algonquin migration and drove a wedge in it which could not be dislodged.

Schoolcraft thinks it probable that the Pequots, who, in the beginning of the seventeenth century were in the ascendency in the Mohican federation, were true Mohicans, and that the wars waged between Sassacus the Pequot and Uncas the Mohican were family rows for the sovereignty of the federation. In speaking of the Pequot war in which that tribe, with its six or seven hundred fighting men, was wiped out he says, "By this defeat the Mohicans, a minor branch of the federation, under the government of Uncas gained the ascendency in Connecticut." The whole matter of tribal relations is so much in doubt that speculation is almost useless, and yet it has a fascination that makes it difficult to leave.

Major Daniel Gookin, who commanded the Middlesex regiment in King Philip's war, writing in 1674, which would be just before that war broke out, enumerates as the five principal "nations" of New England, the "Pequots, including the Mohicans, and occupying the eastern part of the state of Connecticut; the Narragansetts, occupying nearly all of Rhode Island; the Pawkunnawkuts or Wampanoags, chiefly within the jurisdiction of Plymouth Colony; the Massachusetts, in the bay of that name and adjacent parts; and the Pawtuckets north and east of the Massachusetts, including the Pennacooks of New Hampshire, and probably all the northeastern tribes as far as the Abenakis or Tarrateens, as they seem to have been called by the

New England Indians." The Nipmucks he mentions as living north of the Mohicans and west of the Massachusetts, occupying the central part of that state, and acknowledging to a certain extent, the supremacy of the Massachusetts, the Narragansetts or the Mohicans. Other writers also assert that some of their tribes were tributary to the Wampanoags, and there is very good reason for believing this to be true.

These federations comprise the tribes with which the earliest colonists were brought directly in contact, and, consequently in the pursuit of the subject in which we are particularly interested, further mention of the Indians of New England will be limited for the most part to them. In passing, however, a glance at some of the other tribes whom Gookin groups as Abenakis or Tarrateens, will not be out of place.

Other writers apply the term Abenaki to a much narrower limit, confining it to the Micmacs of Nova Scotia, called Souriquois by the French, the Abenaki, now called the St. Francis, in Canada, and the Passamaquoddies and Penobscots of Maine, which four tribes or federations are said to have called themselves not Abenaki, that being the name of one of them, but "Wabanaki," an Algonquin word meaning white or light, and believed to refer to the fact that they were the first upon whom the light of the sun rested as he started in his daily journey across the heavens.

The Micmacs, Passamaquoddies and Penobscots appear to have been extremely rich in folklore,

myth and legend, an interesting collection of which
was made by Charles G. Leland in 1884 under the
title of "Algonquin Legends of New England." As
one of the sources of his authority for these legends
and traditions, Leland tells us that the Wampum
Records of the Passamaquoddies were read for him
by "Sapiel Selmo, the only living Indian who had
the key to them."

Whatever subdivisions may have existed among
them, or whatever federations made up of various
closely related tribes; whatever potency there may
have been in their totemic bonds; whatever civil
wars may have rent them asunder, this fact we
know, that from the time of our earliest knowledge
of this part of the world after the Saga of Thorvald,
until their practical extermination, all of New England was peopled by tribes of this great Algonquin
family. To attempt an enumeration of them would
be useless; their name is legion; and most of them
are long since forgotten, except as they have left
their names indelibly stamped upon the places they
once inhabited, the mountains from whose summits
their watch fires burned as they surveyed from the
lofty heights the country round, and the streams
upon whose silvery bosoms they paddled their
light canoes

A few of the more powerful tribes, or, in some
cases, federations, have made such an impress upon
the life of the colonists, with whom the history of
America, as it is today, begins, that their names
and exploits have been handed down to us by the
writers of that history; and a remnant of what was

once a proud and powerful people in some few cases remains to remind their conquerors how futile were the efforts of the children of nature to withstand the onward sweep of a higher civilization than they had attained. Among the latter are the Passamaquoddies, some five or six hundred of whom still occupy a small portion of their ancient hunting grounds in eastern Maine; the Penobscots, who in the early part of the seventeenth century occupied the beautiful valley of the river and the shores of the bay from which time has not been able to efface their name, and in which river two islands still furnish a home for the five or six hundred remaining members of the tribe; and the Gay Heads, the descendants of the tribe that under the Sachem Epenow, in the Pilgrims' time occupied Capawack or Nope, now Martha's Vineyard, together with a few scattering members of other tribes distributed throughout Massachusetts; to say nothing of the few hundred descendants of the Mohicans who fought under Uncas, and a like number in whose veins flows the blood of the warriors who followed the three great Narragansett Chiefs, Canonicus, Miantonomo and Canonchet.

Many of these have by intermarriage almost lost their identity, and even those who still cling to the lands allotted to them by the governments, are for the most part so crossed with other races that they would not, in most instances, be recognized as the descendants of the men our fathers found here three hundred years ago.

The Passamaquoddies and Penobscots are as

much French as Indian, and nearly all the natives of Massachusetts have mingled the blood of the Indian with that of the African, Schoolcraft saying in 1850 that there were not more than seven or eight full blooded Indians among the eight hundred and forty-seven in the state. Occasionally one meets a family who would never be suspected of being anything but the purest whites, but who boast the blood of the children of the forest.

Among the tribes that have left their names indelibly stamped upon the localities in which they lived, but were not so closely connected with the earliest settlements as to have been active participants in the scenes enacted there, and consequently have not received the particular attention of historians, and have left no sufficient surviving remnant of their former strength to perpetuate their memory through their posterity, one notes with interest the Kennebecs, whose lordly river still flows down to the sea through their ancient hunting grounds with the same calm and peaceful movement in the seasons of low water, and the same torrential rush when the sun in his northward travels unfetters its thousand feeding brooks and springs, as in the days when the children of the forest dipped their dusky bodies in its cooling waters; the Norridgewocks, who dwelt farther back towards the headwaters of the same river, and whose name will not be forgotten as long as the people of Norridgewock, Maine, tell their children that their town derives its name from the Indians whose children listened to the folklore and songs of their people at their mothers' knees on this same spot three centuries ago; the Androscoggins who dipped their paddles noiselessly into the waters of the noble river that now turns the wheels of hundreds of mills, but will not allow the name of its first navigators to be sunk in oblivion; the Piscataquas who dwelt about the place where now a government navy yard gives shelter to men of war beside which the frail bark canoes of the natives are as the fingerlings of the shore beside the leviathans of the deep, and who have left their name upon the river that "widens to meet the sea" at Portsmouth; and the Pemaquids, who little dreamed when they heaped the shells of clams and other edible mollusks in huge piles along the shore, that they were erecting a monument to themselves, to be gazed at in wonder by generations of their destroyers; and whose name still clings to the places they once roamed at will.

Other powerful federations there were whose friendship or hostility were matters of life or death to hundreds, aye, even thousands of the early adventurers who attempted to establish upon these shores homes for themselves and their posterity, adventurers only in the sense that they ventured everything, even life itself, upon a throw of the dice of fate. Drake speaks of five great Sachemries, the Pequots, Narragansetts, Wampanoags, Massachusetts, and Pawtuckets, and he speaks of them as though they were the only five federations in New England worthy the dignity of that designation, following Gookin in this respect; but it may be doubted whether some of these ever held in complete subordination many of the tribes which were at times closely associated with them. An illustration of this is seen in the Connecticut River Indians of various tribal designations, the Mohicans and Niantics who were among the deadly enemies of the Pequots, by whom they were conquered and reduced to such a state of subjugation that they may perhaps have been fairly counted as of the Pequot nation in the early colonial days.

The Tarratines. — Another interesting group whose identity is not clearly established, is that known in New England history as Tarratines, Tarrateens or Tarrentines, as the name is variously spelled. Who they were or whence they came is one of history's unsolved problems. That they were able to muster powerful raiding parties is clearly shown by the success with which they carried out their plundering expeditions against the tribes of Massachusetts and Wampanoags before the pestilence had decimated these two federations. That they were raiders and plunderers is clearly established by the testimony of contemporary writers, part of whose information was gleaned from the sufferers from their expeditions. The great invasion of Massachusetts and Wampanoag territories sometime between 1615 and 1617 is accepted as a historical fact; Bradford speaks of the Massachusetts being in fear of them in September, 1621, that being the season of their visitations to "reap where they have not sowed"; and Drake tells of an attack made by them upon the Indians at Agawam (Ipswich) in August, 1631, in which they killed seven.

In the Planters' Plea they are spoken of as a predatory tribe living fifty or sixty leagues to the northeast (of Massachusetts Bay); and it is there said that they raised no corn on account of the climate, but came down and reaped the Massachusetts Indians' harvest. Drake speaks of them as lying east of the Pawtuckets, and also as lying east of the Piscataqua River, which would place them almost anywhere in Maine, as he does not attempt to give their precise limits. Albert Gallatin in his Archaeologia Americana, in which he calls the five federations of Southern New England by the general designation New England Indians, says the dividing line between these latter and the Abenaki was somewhere between the Piscataqua and the Kennebec, and cites Governor Sullivan as authority for placing it at the Saco River. He also calls attention to what he calls a confirmation of this by French writers who mention a tribe which they call the Sakokies, adjacent to the Abenaki and the New England Indians, and which was originally in alliance with the Iroquois, but were converted by the Jesuits and withdrew into Canada. Other writers locate the Tarratines definitely east of the Penobscot, which would bring them between the Passamaquoddies and the Penobscots unless they were, indeed, roving members of one or both of these tribes. Gallatin makes no other mention of them as a tribe than to quote from Gookin, who speaks of the "Abenakis or Tarrateens, as they are called by the New England Indians." The two names are used by Gookin to designate all the Indians east of the Pawtuckets, and Schoolcraft accepts this classification. Gallatin further says: "The tribes of Nova Scotia in the Bay of Fundy were first called by the French Souriquois. They are now known as Micmacs. The French adopted the names given by the Souriquois to the neighboring tribes. The Etchemins, stretching from the Passamaquoddy Bay to St. John's Island and west of the Kennebec River as far as Cape Cod, they called the Almouchiquois."

Etchemins means canoe men, and may well have been applied to the bold canoe men of all the shore tribes who navigated the deep waters of the sea, and Almouchiquois would then mean the same. If we attempt to give it any other meaning we are forced to the conclusion that the French or the Micmacs, whichever first defined their limits as above, knew very little about the people to the southwest, or that every one else is very much mistaken. Continuing Gallatin says: "The Indians at the mouth of the Kennebec planted nothing according to Champlain, but those further inland or up the river planted maize. These inland tribes were the Abenakis, consisting of several tribes, the principal of which were the Penobscots, the Norridgewocks and the Ameriscoggins, and it is not improbable that the Indians at the mouth of both rivers were confounded by Champlain with the Etchemins belonging to the same nation. The Etchemins comprise the Passamaquoddies in the United States and the St. John's in New Brunswick." In another paragraph he says that Champlain found no cultivation of the soil from Passamaquoddy Bay to the Kennebec River.

The French writers' reference to a tribe between the Abenaki and the New England Indians is interesting from two points. They were in alliance with the Iroquois, which leads to the inquiry whether they may not have been a branch of that group, sprung from some of their war parties who overcame the tribe occupying the location where the French found them, slaughtered the warriors, and took the women to their own wigwams, and settled down upon the conquered territory. Were they the Tarratines? The warlike propensity of the Iroquois manifests itself in the Tarratine raids; but against this theory is the fact that the Iroquois were advanced agriculturalists, and the "Tarratines raised no corn"; and the further fact that the region where nothing was planted was at the mouth of the Kennebec and east of it, while this mysterious tribe, which appears to have escaped the notice of the English writers, lived west of that river. I do not advance any opinion, but simply call attention to this matter as an interesting subject for speculation.

If we attempt to reconcile all the apparently conflicting statements concerning these people, we are forced to the conclusion that the Etchemins or Almouchiquois were the dwellers along the coast, experts in handling their frail barks, daring navigators of various tribes, but not a distinct tribe; that Abenaki was a term applied generally to a large group of tribes covering Maine, New Brunswick and Nova Scotia, the name undoubtedly being de-

rived from the same root as "Wabanaki" which as
already noted means light; that Tarratine was not
the name of any tribe but a term applied to the raiding parties which visited the Massachusetts coast;
and if the statement in the Planter's Plea that they
planted no corn is correct, and Champlain's definite
location of the people who planted nothing is reliable, then the Tarratines were Abenaki, living
east of the Kennebec River or at its mouth; they
were Etchemins, or bold navigators; they planted
nothing, not as said in the Planter's Plea "on account of the climate," for the tribes "farther inland
cultivated maize"; but because they preferred to
secure their supply of corn by reaping their neighbors' harvest.

The Pennacooks. — Gookin, Drake and Schoolcraft speak of the federation, sometimes called Pennacooks, as Pawtuckets, but in his last speech,
Passaconaway, their sachem, uses the term Pennacooks in such a way as to indicate that this was the
name applied to all his people. It may, however,
be that Passaconaway or some of his predecessors,
was originally the sachem of the Pennacooks, and
that this was the dominant tribe in the Pawtucket
federation, just as appears to have been the situation with relation to the Pokanokets and the Wampanoags. As we shall not have occasion again to
refer particularly to the Pennacooks, a word about
its aged sachem, Passaconaway, and his son and
successor, Wonolancet, may well be written here in
passing. Passaconaway resided at Pawtucket Falls
(Lowell), had an alliance with the Penobscots, and

was a friend of Eliot, the celebrated preacher among the Indians, but did not appear to be particulary interested in the religion he preached until 1648. It appears that in 1642, the settlers, becoming distrustful of Passaconaway in consequence of rumors that he was stirring up discord among the Indians, sent men to arrest him and his son Wonolancet. Passaconaway succeeded in evading them through the intervention of a storm that raged with considerable violence, but they took Wonolancet and led him away with a rope around his neck, for by such acts they sought to inspire terror in the hearts of the natives rather than, by acts of consideration, to inspire confidence. Wonolancet escaped but was retaken and brought to Boston. This act made Passaconaway suspicious of the English and of their motives, and undoubtedly served to widen the breach between the two races that had already resulted from some arbitrary acts on the part of the English, and which finally culminated in King Philip's war; and it is given by some early writers as a reason for Passaconaway's refusal to see Eliot when he made a visit to the Falls in the fishing season of 1647. The following year, however, he heard him preach, and publicly announced his belief in the God of the English.

In 1660 he turned over the active direction of the affairs of his tribe to Wonolancet, his son, and soon after died, it is said at the age of one hundred and twenty years. Wonolancet wielded the sceptre until 1667 and maintained friendly relations with the whites during all that time. In 1660, probably on

the occasion of his surrendering the tomahawk of
authority to Wonolancet, a great feast was given at
Pawtucket Falls in his honor, which was attended
not only by his own people but by chiefs and warriors from other tribes. On this occasion, he delivered his farewell address as reported by early
writers as follows:

PASSACONAWAY'S SPEECH

"Hearken to the words of your father! I
am an old oak that has withstood the
storms of more than a hundred winters.
Leaves and branches have been stripped
from me by the winds. My eyes are dim;
my limbs totter; I must soon fall. When
young, no one could bury the hatchet in the
sapling before me. My arrows could pierce
the deer at a hundred rods. No wigwam
had so many furs, no pole had so many
scalplocks as Passaconaway's. Then I delighted in war. The whoop of the Pennacooks was heard on the Mohawk, and no
voice as loud as Passaconaway's. The
scalps upon the pole in my wigwam told
the story of Mohawk suffering. The English came; they seized the lands; they followed upon my footpaths. I made war
upon them but they fought with fire and
thunder. My young men were swept down
before me when no one was near them. I
tried sorcery against them but they still in-

creased, and prevailed over me and mine; I gave place to them and retired to my beautiful island, Naticook. I, who can take the rattlesnake in my palm as I would a worm without harm — I, that have had communication with the Great Spirit, dreaming and awake — I am powerless before the pale faces. These meadows they shall turn with the plow; these forests shall fall by the axe; the pale faces shall live upon your hunting grounds and make their villages upon your fishing places. The Great Spirit says this and it must be so. We are few and powerless before them. We must bend before the storm. Peace with the white men is the command of the Great Spirit and the wish — the last wish — of Passaconaway."

I have already referred to the Leni Lenapee as the parent stock of the Algonquins; and to the fact of their subjugation by the Five Nations at some time between 1649 and 1672; but as I did not call attention to the depth of their degradation, this chapter would hardly be complete without furthur reference to it. So complete was their defeat and submission to their conquerors, that they were compelled to forego the use of arms and to assume the name of "women." So when Penn made his famous treaty with them in 1682, he treated with "women" and not with warriors.

When the Five Nations afterwards allotted land

to them, and they were crowded by the encroachments of settlers, they moved even further west than they were ordered, and espoused the cause of the French in their wars with the English.

At the outbreak of the revolution they declared their independence of their conquerors, and a few years later at a public council, the Five Nations confessed that the Lenapee were no longer women but men; and thus the stock that had peopled nearly all the north-eastern part of the continent came into its own again. At the time of which we write they had not been reduced to a state of vassalage. but were still the grandfather of the other tribes of the Algonquin family and lived in their ancient hunting grounds, a free people, just as their descendants lived in all the vast territory the limits of which I have already outlined.

Here they and their children of the other tribes fished the streams whose banks are now lined with the cities of the strangers from across the great waters whom they welcomed with open arms, and who repaid their hospitality by waging upon them a perpetual war of extermination. Here they hunted the primeval forests, which the settlers' axe has laid low that the giant trees might contribute to the requirements of a people to whom the Indian methods of living were but a tradition of the past. Here, too, their war whoops resounded as they waged their internecine war upon each other; and here, when the tomahawk had been buried, they smoked the pipe of peace, and its smoke ascending wafted their prayers to the Great Spirit, whose existence revealed itself to them in every object that came within range of their observation.

The Wampanoags, Narragansetts, Pequots and Mohicans were so closely associated with the various affairs growing out of the first contact of the whites with Massasoit and his Wampanoags that I shall consider them further in subsequent chapters, which will also contain occasional reference to the Massachusetts; and, as the individuality of the sachems was a potent factor in the attitude of their tribes, due attention will be given to the prominent leaders of their people.

IV

THE WAMPANOAGS

DECEMBER 7, 1620 (December 17, new style) found the *Mayflower* lying inside of Cape Cod. This locality, and particularly "the place that on Captain John Smith's map is called Plimoth," had been highly recommended to them as a suitable location for the establishment of a permanent settlement. They had been on shipboard for a long time, the life was becoming irksome, and they were desirous of effecting a landing before the Sabbath which was approaching, and on which, in their religious zeal, there could be no question of work. So they sent their shallop ashore in search of a suitable spot. The shallop made a landing at Nauset, now Eastham, a place which derived its name from that of the tribe of Indians located there, which we find mentioned frequently in the writings of the early chroniclers. The boat's crew spent the night there, and in the early morning they were alarmed by the sentry whom they had posted, and who announced the presence of Indians. This alarm was followed by a demonstration against the camp. The natives were soon driven off by the discharge of the muskets of the English, who then returned to their ship. After this, their first encounter with the aboriginal inhabitants of the land, they were not further annoyed by them until the following February, when they began to show themselves from time to time about the settlement at Plymouth, always holding themselves aloof, however, until the sixteenth of March, when Samoset made his memorable visit with the details of which every reader of American history is familiar.

Colonel Robert B. Caverly in his account of the early Indian wars speaks of Aspinet, who was sachem of Nauset at that time, as a Mohandsick. The people of this name were located on Long Island and the question naturally arises, how came this detached tribe of Mohandsicks, whose war strength in 1621 was said to be one hundred warriors, to be so separated from the rest of their kindred? The Mohandsicks, like the Manhattans of lower New York, probably were Mohicans, or at least more closely related to the latter than to any other of the numerous branches of the Algonquin family; and, while it does not appear that there had been any hostility between the Mohicans and the Wampanoags, perhaps because of the fact that their hunting grounds were separated by those of the Narragansetts, it seems rather out of the ordinary course that we would expect migrations to take for this tribe to separate itself from the remainder of its people and isolate itself down on the end of Cape Cod in Wampanoag territory. There would be but two ways for them to have reached that point, one by water, which with their limited facilities for making such long journeys seems imprac-

ticable, though not impossible, and the other by
crossing Narragansett and Wampanoag territory,
which could be done only if they were on friendly
terms; unless, indeed, they were a detached body of
Mohandsicks, who had settled on the mainland very
early in the period of migration and had been swept
down to the extreme end of the Cape by succeeding
waves, and had there been able to maintain themselves, or had been allowed to remain unmolested.

None of these theories is impossible, as we have
seen the Tuscaroras separating themselves from the
other nations of the Iroquois and, either crossing
leagues of Algonquin territory, or following the
coast in their frail canoes, settling on the coast of
the Carolinas.

Whatever may have been the most intimate
racial connection of the Nausets, there can be no
doubt that at the time of which I am writing, they
were subjects of the Great Sachem of the Wampanoags, although, as we shall see hereafter, they did
not hesitate at times to engage in conspiracies
against the whites without the sanction of their
great chief. It may be that other tribes in the
eastern part of the Wampanoag domain, such as the
Manomets, Monamoyicks, Paomets, Sawkattuckets,
Matakes, Nobsquossets, and Sokones, and perhaps
the Nantuckets and the Capawacks, were more
closely related to the Nausets than to the western
tribes of the Wampanoag federation, which seem to
have centered about the Pokanokets. They were
all Algonquins, and probably, originally all of the
Totem of the Wolf, the various subdivisions result-

ing from the spreading out process by which a group became separated from the parent stock, thus forming a nation within the family, and eventually acquiring a distinct dialect; and no doubt, in many instances, absorbing tribes that had originally formed a part of some other wave of migration, and so belonged to some other nation.

In any event, the Nausets, with all the other tribes on the cape and the islands, were, to all intents and purposes, Wampanoags at the time of their demonstration against the crew of the shallop on December 8, 1620; and so it was the Wampanoags who first greeted the Pilgrims, though the greeting was far from being a welcome, the actual welcome being extended nearly three months later by a sagamore of Monhigan "two days' sail with a strong wind" to the northeast.

If our conclusion as to the reasonable inferences to be drawn from the writings of early historians is correct, this would place him in the group designated by Gookin, Drake, and Schoolcraft as Abenaki.

Reference has already been made in general terms to the location of the Wampanoags as described by Gookin and Drake, but some doubt exists as to the exact extent of their territory. All are agreed that they held sway from the Islands and Cape Cod to Narragansett Bay and Providence River, and from the Atlantic Ocean north to the southern boundary of the Massachusetts, who as we have seen lived around the bay that bears their name. Just where that boundary ran is not clear, but it is certain that the counties of Nantucket, Dukes, Barnstable, Plymouth, Bristol, and a considerable part of Norfolk, in Massachusetts, together with all of Bristol and Newport counties and the town of East Providence in Rhode Island have been carved out of the ancient hunting grounds of the Wampanoags.

Colonel Caverly, who has written a very interesting account of the early Indian wars in New England, seems to extend the territory or dominion of the Wampanoags much further than any other writer with whose works I am familiar, and further, I fear, than there is any well grounded warrant for, as he speaks of the Massachusetts as being of that federation, as though the fact were established beyond peradventure, and at least suggests that Massasoit's rule extended to and covered the Pennacooks, speaking of Passaconaway as holding sway "under, from and after Massasoit, from the Penobscot to the Merrimack." As we have already seen, Gookin, who wrote only fifty-three years after the landing of the Pilgrims, speaks of the Massachusetts and the Pawtuckets or Pennacooks as independent federations, and it is probable that their relations with the Wampanoags were nothing more than those of allies.

Great as is the uncertainty concerning the exact limits of their territory, their numerical strength at the time of the landing of the Pilgrims is wrapped in even greater obscurity and doubt. Two recent events, however, had reduced them to a mere vestige of their former power. The first of these was a raid of the Tarratines, the conflicting opinions of whose identity and location I have attempted to reconcile in part in the preceding chapter.

The exact location of the Tarratines is of interest at this time only as it directs our attention to the distances which they traveled in making their raids upon the Massachusetts coast; one hundred and fifty to one hundred and eighty miles by water, and much further by land. If the raids were made by water, as seems probable, it certainly shows the Tarratines to have been daring navigators, when one considers the character of their craft, as far as known. It is recorded by men who received their information at first hand that they swept down on the coast tribes of eastern Massachusetts in 1615 or 1616 and inflicted severe losses upon them. These tribes were of the Massachusetts and Wampanoags, and while the extent of the ravages of the invaders is not certainly known, there is no doubt that this raid considerably weakened these two federations, as it is claimed by some that they swept clear across the Wampanoag country and attacked the Narragansetts. This method of securing a livelihood by wresting from their neighbors the fruits of their toil rather than by relying exclusively upon their own systematic efforts to sustain themselves by the pursuit of the usual vocations of their kind, hunting, fishing and the crude cultivation of the soil, appears to have been characteristic of them, for Bradford records the fact that on September 18, 1621, the Plymouth settlers sent out their shallop with ten men, and Squanto as guide to trade with the Massachusetts, and to explore the bay; that they accomplished their purpose and "found kind entertainment. The people were much afraid of the Tarrentines, a people to the eastward which used to come in harvest time and take away their corne, and many times kill their persons."

The second, and by far more disastrous visitation that ravaged the land of the Wampanoags, was a devastating pestilence which followed close on the heels of the Tarratine raid, and worked such havoc among the natives, who had no skill to combat it, that the early visitors from Plymouth to Massasoit's town Sowams, speak of seeing their bones in large numbers scattered along the route, the living not being able to bury the dead. The Patuxet tribe which had occupied the territory around Plymouth, was almost entirely wiped out by this plague, the exact character of which has never been definitely determined. While there is no doubt that the Wampanoags were reduced by these two agencies to a mere shadow of their former strength and power, there is so much conflict between the writers of old times concerning their numbers at the time of the landing of the Pilgrims that we are left almost entirely to conjecture concerning the matter. Certain facts, however, have been handed down upon such reliable authority, that perhaps a careful consideration of those indisputable facts will justify us in making our own estimate; and this leads us to an examination of the extreme claims. I am unable to find that any contemporary writers have left any word from which we would be justified in assuming that anything like an accurate estimate of their

numbers was ever made or attempted by the early
colonists; so perhaps we may fairly conclude that
the truth of the matter lies somewhere between the
two extremes. Some authors, who put out their
works with the intent to convey exact information
to their readers, tell us that this federation numbered not more than three hundred in 1620, having
been reduced to this state from a former strength
variously estimated at anywhere from eighteen
thousand to thirty thousand, their five thousand
warriors mentioned by some, leaning towards the
higher rather than the lower of these two figures.
This three hundred may be construed in so many
ways that before rejecting it as an absurdity, it may
be well to consider to what the number may have
referred. If by it is meant the entire numerical
strength of the federation, it seems to be capable
of complete refutation, and, on the other hand, if
it is limited to the warriors rather than the entire
tribal membership, it is open to grave doubt. Another view is that it may have been intended to be
confined to the village where their Great Sachem
maintained his lodge, or to the three villages between
which he seems to have divided a large part of his
time. Before proceeding to a more general discussion of the numerical strength of the tribe or federation, let us look for a moment at these three villages.
We find Massasoit sometimes spoken of as the Sachem of the Pokanokets. Pokanoket is or was the
geographical name of all that territory now included in the towns of Bristol, Warren, Barrington
and East Providence, Rhode Island, and parts of

Swansea, Rehoboth and Seekonk, Massachusetts.
The Great Sachem seems to have had a more intimate connection with this portion of his domain
than with other parts; and while the tribes in other
localities had their sub-sachems or sagamores, who
acknowledged some sort of allegiance to the Great
Chief, there is nothing from which we would be
justified in inferring that the Pokanokets were under
the direction or control of any of these secondary
chiefs; and it may well be that the Great Sachem
of the Wampanoags either in Massasoit's early days,
or in the time of some of his predecessors, was
simply the sachem of the Pokanokets, with hunting
grounds limited to the territory already defined;
and that at some time a federation of related,
neighboring and conquered tribes was formed under
the name Wampanoag, and that he retained the
government of his original tribe, and governed the
other tribes through their sachems. It would be
extremely interesting reading for us of later generations if some savant of the early colonial period
could have sufficiently secured the confidence of the
contemporary mystery men of the aborigines to
have learned from them the secrets which their
predecessors "talked into the sacred wampum records" and thus handed down from father to son.
From such sources much of historic value might
have been learned for transmission to posterity,
much more than the world knows of Indian legend
and tradition. But the men who came here came
not as seekers after knowledge concerning the character of the country, its geological formations, its

plants, its animals, or its primitive human deni-
zens, and most of the information that has been
gleaned along the latter lines, has come from the
legends and traditions passed along by the natives
to the whites at later dates after the tribes into
whose past we endeavor to penetrate through the
dark clouds of obscurity and doubt had been almost
or quite exterminated. So while the plants and
flowers, the rocks and the wild animals have remained to tell their own story, unfortunately, we
are left in darkness concerning many of the things
we fain would know about the primitive race that
has been swept away by the invaders. We are left
largely to conjecture; and can only draw what
seem to us to be reasonable inferences from known
facts. In the Pokanoket country, there were three
principal villages all of which are sometimes mentioned as Massasoit's dwelling places, and in and
about which he undoubtedly spent more of his time
than in other parts of his domain, although he unquestionably resorted to the other portions for
hunting and fishing and for conferences with his sub-
sachems. These three villages were Sowams, probably where Warren now stands, although some place
it farther west, and their contention seems to be
supported by an ancient map; but Gen. Guy Fessenden and Virginia Baker have made out such a
strong case for the Warren site that I do not propose to enter into any further discussion of the
question; Montaup, corrupted by the English into
Mount Hope in Bristol, Rhode Island; and Kicke-
muit on the river of the same name, and within the

limits of the present town of Swansea, Massachusetts.

Let us now return to a further consideration of the numerical strength of the Wampanoags in the early part of the seventeenth century; and, having referred briefly to what we may properly consider the minimum estimate, we will pass to the other extreme, and then by examining all the known facts, see what appears to be the reasonable conclusion to be drawn from those facts, not for the purpose of ascertaining an accurate estimate, which could be of no particular benefit, but for the purpose of properly appraising the value of the friendship of Massasoit to the early settlers; for it must be apparent that that value would be determined in part by his strength and standing among the various tribes. We may well begin this line of inquiry by taking the testimony of Captain Thomas Dermer, master of a vessel sailing here for trade and exploration. Captain Dermer was on the New England coast in 1619, probably not for the first time. It was with him that Squanto returned to his native land after spending some years in England. In 1619, with Squanto as interpreter, he traveled inland to Nemasket, now Middleboro, Massachusetts, where he held an interview with two "Kings of Pokanoket" of which we shall see more hereafter. In a letter to a friend dated June 20, 1620, Dermer wrote that "Squanto was carried away from a place that on Captain John Smith's map is called Plimoth," and that "the Pocanawits" (Pokanokets) "which live to the west of Plimoth bear an in-

veterate malice to the English, and are of more
strength than all the savages from thence to the
Penobscote." Dermer must have secured this
knowledge from some of the natives, and it may
not be amiss to inquire into the possible sources of
his information and the time. To begin with the
latter, I call particular attention to the date of the
letter and to Dermer's voyage in 1619 and his probable earlier trips to the New World. He had undoubtedly come in contact with the various tribes
along the coast from whom he may have learned
about the Pokanokets; and he brought Squanto
with him in 1619 or on an earlier expedition.
Squanto spoke English and was a member of one
of the small tribes of the Wampanoag federation, so
it is extremely probable that Dermer's information
came from him. Squanto was carried away in 1614
before the pestilence had decimated the tribes of
eastern Massachusetts, and if the information was
secured from this source, it may have referred to conditions as Squanto knew them before he left these
parts. This is especially likely to have been the
case if Squanto first came over with Dermer in
1619 and had no knowledge of the ravages of the
plague. On the other hand, if Dermer remained
long in this vicinity at the time of his visit to Nemasket, he must have learned of these ravages, and
the combined strength of all the tribes of the Wampanoags may then have been as great as he says in
his letter of June 20, 1620. There is one important
fact that lends color to this theory, and that is
that the voyage inland to Nemasket was from

Plymouth, the Patuxet of Squanto, and he, finding his own tribe wiped out, would undoubtedly have ascertained the cause on arriving at Nemasket, even if he had met no one to give him the information before.

However that may have been, we cannot doubt the testimony of Bradford who writes that on March 16, 1621, Samoset, after welcoming the English to Patuxet, and being entertained by them over night, told them of a Great Sachem, "Massasoyt," who had sixty warriors under him, and left them saying he would bring him to them. On March 22, the Great Chief appeared with the exact number mentioned by Samoset.

In the June following, when Winslow and Hopkins visited him at Sowams for the purpose of renewing and strengthening the ties of friendship between him and the colonists and to secure corn for planting, Massasoit, speaking to an assembly of his own people, said, "Am not I Massasoit commander of the country round you? Is not such a town mine, and such a town, and will you not bring your skins to the English?" In this way naming more than thirty villages, according to Winslow.

We have already seen that on December 8, 1620, the Nausets attacked the crew of the *Mayflower's* shallop, and, while the numbers of the attacking party are not mentioned, there can be no doubt, from Bradford's description, that they were in sufficient force to make a considerable demonstration and cause great alarm and uneasiness, and Samoset is said to have told the English that Aspinet had one

hundred warriors. In addition to the inhabitants of
the Pokanoket country and the Nausets, both of
which we have briefly discussed, there is abundant
evidence that there were tribes of no mean propor-
tions at Capawack (Martha's Vineyard), Manomet
and Monamoyick, Sawkattucket, Nobsquosset and
Matakes, besides that on Nantucket Island, in the
eastern part of Massasoit's domain; at Assawamsett, and Nemasket, at Sakonnet at the mouth of the
river of the same name, and at Pocasset, or perhaps
it would be more accurate to say in the Sakonnet
territory and the Pocasset territory, for the former
extended over the southern part of Tiverton and all
of Little Compton, Rhode Island, and the latter,
lying immediately east of the Pokanoket territory,
extended from Coles River in Swansea eastward at
least four miles beyond the Taunton River, and
from the narrows in the Sakonnet River, where the
Tiverton Stone Bridge now stands, northward to
the northern boundary of Freetown, including part
of Tiverton, Rhode Island, all of Fall River, most
of Freetown, and parts of Berkley, Dighton, Somerset and Swansea, Massachusetts. The Chief of this
tribe was Corbitant, of whom we shall see more
later, who resided at "Mettapuyst" (Mettapoissett)
now Gardner's Neck in Swansea. All of these were
probably included in Massasoit's enumeration of
"more than thirty villages," and particular attention is called to them at this time, because there is
reason for believing that they were fairly powerful
tribes, and all within the Wampanoag federation. I
have not directed particular attention to the Massa-

chusetts, because there may be some question of their relation to the Wampanoags, whether they were of them or only allied with them, the weight of the evidence pointing rather to the latter idea than to the former; and I have disregarded entirely Colonel Caverly's statement concerning Passaconaway as previously adverted to; nor have I made any reference to the tribes of the Nipmucks who were subject to the Great Chief of the Wampanoags.

A careful consideration of what has been said is sufficient to lead to the conclusion that the three hundred mentioned by some writers as all that remained of the thirty thousand Wampanoags that escaped the plague must have referred to the warriors of Pokanoket alone, or the inhabitants of Massasoit's village of Sowams. It is hardly possible to have mustered the sixty warriors who accompanied him to Plymouth from a total tribal membership scattered from the Cape and Islands to the Providence River, as must have been done if the entire population was only three hundred; and it is not probable that Massasoit would leave his women and children totally unguarded in the presence of the none too friendly Narragansetts across the river, who according to some historians had in comparatively recent years taken advantage of his reduced power to wage war upon him, and had wrested from him his beautiful island of Aquidnick. The distance from Sowams to Plymouth by the old Indian trail is said by early writers to have been forty miles, and the three days, at least, required for the journey out and back, and for the conference, would be a long time to leave his village unguarded if the Narragansetts had happened to make a raid at that time. What probably happened was this. Starting out on an expedition the outcome of which was problematical, Massasoit most likely took the "panieses," or men of valor, of the three villages already mentioned. These would undoubtedly be the most vigorous and active of the men who formed the war council, and, at the same time, were the warriors who followed him and were under his immediate command when on the war path, the warriors of the other tribes of the federation being under the immediate command of their sachems. If this theory is correct, it lends color to the inference that the three hundred comprised simply the population of Sowams, or the warriors of Pokanoket; and it may well be that the writers who have placed this estimate on the numerical strength of the Wampanoags, taking into account the well known fact that every place of considerable importance had its sub-sachem or sagamore, may have looked upon the people of Sowams, or possibly of Sowams and the territory immediately surrounding it, as all there was of the true Wampanoags; but I am inclined to believe that this name is simply the appelation of a confederacy of which the Pokanokets was the dominant tribe, and which was held together in part by the strength of that tribe, and in part by the necessity of combining to prevent the inroads of invading enemies. There undoubtedly also existed some closer bond of relationship, closer family ties perhaps, among most of the federated tribes than

between them and other branches of the great
Algonquin family, or in other words a true Wampanoag Nation with subject tribes. There is no evidence of a single tribe of this name, unless it was
another name for the Pokanokets. There is another
possibility that should not be overlooked in this
connection, and that is that Massasoit may have
started out with less than the sixty with whom he
arrived at Plymouth and augmented his force on
the way, although it is almost certain that he did
not draw from the Pocassets, because there is very
good reason for supposing that Corbitant, their sachem, was not in sympathy with Massasoit's design
to cultivate the friendship of the English, and it is
equally certain that Corbitant was a chief of such
importance that his presence would have been
noted, had he been of the party. This suggestion is
advanced as a remote possibility, but that it is
hardly more than that is evidenced by the fact that
Samoset spoke of Massasoit as having sixty warriors
under him and that was the number that appeared
with him.

The Pocassets, as we have already seen, formed
one of the most important branches or subdivisions
of the Wampanoag federation. Their exact numerical strength is almost as much in doubt as is
that of the entire branch of the Algonquin family to
which the name "Wampanoag" is applied, although
there is reliable authority for the claim frequently
advanced that Corbitant, their Sachem in 1620,
could muster three hundred warriors, and estimating one warrior to five members of the tribe, this

would give them a total of fifteen hundred, which is probably as near as it is possible to estimate the strength of any of the tribes. They lived in the territory immediately east of the Pokanoket country, and their numbers and close proximity to Massasoit's own tribe, together with the personality of their sachem, furnishes a reason for singling them out for particular mention at this time. Corbitant was a man of considerable importance, as indeed any man who could command three hundred warriors would be in the Wampanoag nation, weakened as it was by the raid of the Tarratines and the plague. He was not always in sympathy with some of Massasoit's moves, and his known hostility and independent scheming naturally lead us to inquire whether the strength of the Wampanoags has not been greatly underestimated by some, the reasonable inference being that Corbitant might quite naturally be expected to lead an open revolt if there had been any chance of success, the natives not being held in check by any doctrine of the divine rights of kings, and not looking upon the persons of their Great Chiefs as being endowed with any particular sanctity. Corbitant, while maintaining friendly relations with the whites apparently did it more as the part of political wisdom than through a desire to encourage and aid them. He was undoubtedly the sachem who was with Massasoit in his sickness in 1623, the day before Winslow arrived at Sowams, and sought to arouse Massasoit's hostility to the English saying as Winslow writes, "if we had been as good friends indeed as we were now

in show, we would have visited him in this his
sickness, using many arguments to withdraw his
affections, and to persuade him to give way to some
things against us, which were motioned to him not
long before." Winslow does not mention the name
of this sachem, but enough is known of Corbitant
to lead to the belief that it was he. On the occasion of this visit to Massasoit, Winslow stopped at
"Mattapuyst" with Corbitant on his way to Sowams; and after his mission was accomplished, and
Massasoit sufficiently recovered so that his friends
returned to their homes, he went to Corbitant's
lodge with him and spent the night there. He
speaks of the Chief as a "notable politician, yet full
of merry jests and squibs, and never better pleased
than when the like are returned upon him." Corbitant was one of the eight sachems who acknowledged themselves subjects of King James
in September 1621, his name being written Caunbitant on that document.

Wamsutta, or Mooanam, Massasoit's oldest son,
married Weetamo, supposed to be the daughter of
Corbitant; and, undoubtedly in right of his wife,
seems to have exercised some authority over the
Pocassets after Corbitant's death. In 1659 he
joined with other Indians in a grant of a tract of
land covering all of what is now Freetown and
more than half of Fall River to twenty-six purchasers who were free men and from whom the
purchase is known in history as the Freemen's purchase. Weetamo is frequently referred to as the
Squaw Sachem of the Pocassets, and we will have

occasion to refer to her again, as well as to the part played by the Pocassets in King Philip's war.

The Wampanoags and the Narragansetts appear to have made more progress towards civilization than most of the other Indian tribes, except possibly the Iroquois League of Northern New York. Massasoit dwelt in a lodge at Sowams of a much more substantial character than the ordinary tepees, and Corbitant undoubtedly had a similar residence at Mettapoisett. There is still shown in the town of Warren the Pokanoket's grist mill, consisting of a natural flat table rock into which grooves have been cut or worn by use, where the women of the tribe ground their corn by rolling round stones over it, these movable stones being operated by rolling them like a wheel about a shaft thrust through a hole drilled in the center. From the meal thus produced they made the Rhode Island Johnny cakes, the counterparts of which still tickle the palates of the descendents of the women who learned the art of making them from the Indian women of almost three centuries ago. The Rhode Island clambake, the mere mention of which is still sufficient to call together a multitude wherever that famous repast is known, had its origin with one or the other of these tribes and was known to both. The Indian method of preparing it is still recognized as the one method that gives it the peculiar flavor that cannot be secured in any other way; that method consisting of heating rocks by building fires upon them, and then removing the embers and placing clams, fish and green corn upon the rocks and covering

them with seaweed to hold the heat until the whole
is thoroughly cooked. Agriculture they had developed to a greater extent than most tribes, for
while their cultivation of the soil was crude, they
adopted artificial fertilization, which they taught to
the whites as we shall hereafter see; and they raised
corn and beans in abundance from which they made
succotash, a dish originating with them; and they
had made some progress in the potter's art. The
Pokanokets constructed on the banks of the Kicke-
muit River a bath to which they resorted for the
cure of the ills that assailed them, and there is reason
for believing that both they and the Narragansetts
had others of a like character in other places. This
bath consisted of a structure built of non-com-
bustible materials or cut in the clay banks, and was
heated in the same manner as that employed in
preparing the clambake for cooking as already outlined. In this building they then sat and smoked
while the perspiration rolled down their dusky
bodies, concluding with a plunge in the river.

Such was the federation that occupied the land
surrounding the place at which that little band of
devoted pilgrims first set foot on the New World.
They had fled from England to Holland that they
might escape the rigorous discipline of the established church, and exercise their own free will in the
matter of religious worship; but Holland was not
their destination; it was simply the place of a tem-
porary sojourn, until the hand of destiny led them
across the dark waters in search of a broader field
of endeavor. We are sometimes impressed with a

belief that they were the instruments of fate sent hither to establish in the newly discovered western hemisphere a new order, out of which, eventually, there was destined to arise a greater freedom, a broader humanity, than the world had before known. It is no wonder that they, in their zeal, speak of their escapes from the extraordinary perils that beset them both on the water in their frail bark, and subsequently on the land, as due to the special dispensation of Divine Providence. Their safe passage of the stormy sea in late autumn; their landing at a place the entire population of which had been wiped out, thus reducing to a minimum the probability of molestation by natives who had no reason to love the English, no reason to look upon them in any light but that of marauders who might without provocation and without warning attack them with their terrible weapons of fire and thunder, or carry them away into slavery as had been done before; and the kindly greeting they received after their first unpleasant encounter with the natives, all conspire to impel us of this more skeptical age to indulge them in attributing this first successful issue of their venture to the intervention of the hand that guided the tribes of Israel through their many tribulations, until, purified by the fire of adversity, they arose triumphant and bore the ark of the covenant into the Promised Land. If there was one thing more than another, or more than all others, that showed the protecting hand of Providence, it was the disposition of the Great Sachem of the Wampanoags and his people to extend to the strangers the right hand of friendship, and to dwell side by side with them in amity for half a century; for until the outbreak of King Philip's war, there was no serious trouble between the whites and the Wampanoags. Minor outbreaks and personal acts of violence there were, but, in general, they lived side by side in peace and security, and while there were discords, suspicions and wars with others, the Wampanoags, under the guiding hand of their Great Sachem Massasoit, remained faithful to their treaty obligations.

V

MASSASOIT

BORN 1580 — DIED 1661

IT is as a man of peace that we know Massasoit, Great Sachem of the Wampanoags. There is nothing in his career as far as it is revealed by the white man's history, to appeal to the fiery ardor and enthusiasm of youth like the exploits of his son Pometacom or Metacomet, the King Philip of history, or Red Jacket, Joseph Brant, Pontiac, Tecumseh or scores of others whose deeds of valor have fired the imagination and thrilled the hearts of our young men for generations; but to the man in middle life, whose blood has been cooled to some extent by the snows of many winters, to the student of human character, there is something about the calm and dignified demeanor of that great chief that brings a feeling of regret that the colonists should have looked upon the continued existence of his race as an insurmountable barrier to the fruition of their ambitious designs, and should have considered it necessary to exterminate a race which by its own unaided efforts, through ages of slow development with no contact with the enlightenment of the old world attained through eons of labored progress, with no guiding hand to assist it in its groping

91

towards the light, had made sufficient advancement along the paths of civilization to produce such a man.

I am aware that the vast majority of the superficial readers of early American history have concluded that the Indian tribes of Massachusetts, Rhode Island and Connecticut were wiped out in a cruel and unprovoked war begun by King Philip in open violation of the treaty his father had made with Governor Carver of the Plymouth Colony; but the man who holds this view cannot have looked into the violations of that treaty by the whites, and takes no account of the long list of aggressions against the natives in violation of the spirit of the treaty if not of its letter. The great cause of that bloody war was the tendency on the part of the colonists to treat the Indians as a subject race to whom they owed no duty, who were in their way, and whom they were at liberty to annoy constantly in every conceivable manner. If they had set out with a determination to arouse the natives to declare war, in order that they might use the hostilities thus begun as an excuse for exterminating them, they could not have succeeded more admirably. When we consider the wonderful sagacity, the political wisdom of Massasoit's move in seeking to establish friendly relations with the invaders of his soil and to pave the way for the two races to live side by side in peace and harmony, instead of sounding the alarm and calling his trusty warriors about him to expel the foreign foe, we cannot fail to be impressed with his foresight, based, as

it was, upon his knowledge of men in a wild and natural state, and unacquainted with the arts and wiles of civilization. That his judgment was in error, and his confidence misplaced was no fault of his, but the misfortune of his people. Had the colonists shown half the regard for the spirit of the treaty they made with him, and for the obligations they thereby assumed towards him and his, that he manifested during the forty years of his life after its signing, what a different story would the annals of New England tell today. It is almost enough to bring the blush of shame to the white man's cheek to recount the story of colonial perfidy towards the friendly Wampanoags and Narragansetts, once the story is stripped of the cant with which it has been decked out and which we have been too accustomed to regard as religious zeal.

Zealots the Pilgrims were, religious fanatics, rivaling the janizaries of the Moslem world, seeking a place where they might enjoy religious freedom and celebrating their success by denying to others the freedom they sought to establish for themselves. They allowed no fine scruples of decency and honor to stand in the way of spurring on to their death a race that seemed to them to be an impediment to their material progress. They converted what they could by preaching the word, and stopped at no savage cruelty to wipe out what they could not convert. Their most eminent divines exulted over the defeat of the men who had been their friends, but whom they had betrayed so often that their friendship had been turned to hostility. The chil-

dren of the forest, following the strongest instinct in
the human breast, and fighting for their own preser-
vation and the protection of home and fireside, were
ruthlessly slaughtered by the men between whom
and annihilation they had interposed their naked
breasts, and whose priests boasted of the number of
souls they "sent to hell" in some battle brought on
by their treatment of the men to whom they had
allied themselves by the most solemn ties. Cant
and hypocrisy have ever gone hand in hand with
excessive religious zeal, and the preachers of New
England furnished, not an exception to the rule, but
its most striking example. They preached the word
of God and pretended to be followers of the humble
Nazarene; but practiced the wiles of the devil; and
rivaled him in their satanic exultation over the fate
of the foes they made by their diabolical practices.

There was bound to be a conflict between European and Indian methods of living. The two could
not co-exist on the same soil. The two races could
not long live side by side except by one of them
conforming to the mode of life of the other. It
was inevitable that the country must be all savage
or all civilized; but there was no danger to European ideals and civilization in trying the experiment
of leavening the whole lump. The Indians of eastern Massachusetts and Rhode Island had shown
sufficient intelligence and sufficient interest in English customs and manners of living to warrant a
hope for a complete reclamation of the race. True
civilization is not of such a quality or character
that it is in danger of being lost by extending it to

cover a broader field than has been its wont. It is a condition that is strengthened and invigorated by propagation and extension. It was no more in danger of extinction in the wilds of New England by bringing the natives within its enlightening influence, than is the light of the sun of being extinguished by turning it into hitherto unexplored regions of darkness.

The Pilgrims brought with them the seed from which, by careful culture, has developed our civil and religious liberty. They planted and nourished it here, even though they were themselves as intolerant of others as were those from whom they fled, of them. It is characteristic of freedom that it grows and flourishes under adversity. The greater the opposition, the stronger the growth, even though temporarily checked by the heavy hand of oppression; and it is unfortunate that the founders of our liberties should have considered it necessary to water the seed they planted with the blood of nature's freemen.

The liberty that cannot flourish without enslaving another is not worth preserving, and the American people through long years of toil and suffering learned this great truth; and, out of the limited freedom established by the colonies, evolved the only true freedom, to move unfettered and untrammelled as far as can be done without interference with the equal liberty of another. If the early settlers on these shores had recognized this eternal truth, instead of leaving it to their posterity to evolve as the true foundation of right and justice, the story of their injustice would never have been told. But all human progress is slow; and as man cannot, by a single bound, reach the mountain top, so a race cannot at once spring from darkness into perfect light.

I would not detract from the stern virtues of the men who laid the foundations of our free institutions, the planters who labored early and late that we might reap for generations in greater measure than was vouchsafed to them; but, remembering that it is easier to sail a charted sea than to thread one's way among the rocks and shoals of an unknown coast, we may still be permitted a measure of criticism of the methods they adopted for the accomplishment of their purpose. Looking back upon the scenes of the long ago, one knows not which most to admire, the pertinacity with which the Christian English clung to the establishment of their ideals, which, illuminated by the ever increasing light of intellectual freedom, have become our ideals; or that of the pagan Indian, who, finding that his liberty was being gradually swallowed up in that which he had helped the English to establish upon his lands, turned at bay and attempted to break the fetters which the English liberty was forging for him and his.

The results of the coming of the Pilgrim fathers have been told in song and story; they have been heralded wherever the voice of men is heard; they have been taught to lisping children at their mothers' knee, and have been the theme of poets and the realization of the dream of philosophers.

I would not gainsay them if I could; I would not turn back the wheels of human progress; I would not dim the lustre of one ray from the torch of liberty our fathers lighted, and which has burned brighter with each succeeding generation until its rays have penetrated the uttermost parts of the earth; but without detracting from the accomplishments of the mighty men of the past, I would do honor to the valiant race which, seeing its liberties endangered by the encroachments of the men whom it had welcomed, sprang to arms for the defence of their freedom, with a zeal that has won our commendation wherever displayed by civilized peoples from Marathon to the Argonne. I would pause in the contemplation of the glories of the past, long enough to deposit a wreath of earth's fairest blossoms upon the places where lie buried the hopes and aspirations of the noblest race of savages the world has ever seen. I would turn aside to look upon Sachem's Plain and Mount Hope with a feeling of regret that the men who fell there could not have devoted their God given energy to the accomplishment of their dreams of living with their white brethren in peace and harmony. A race that could produce a Massasoit is not all bad, and it is a misfortune to the world that the good that was in it could not have developed side by side with the good that our fathers had inherited from the memories of a thousand years of upward struggling towards the light.

The hand of Destiny that planted the seeds of Freedom for you and me, under the erring guidance of those who controlled it for their own benefit, sowed the seeds of death and extermination for the simple natives, who seemed to the blind, unreasoning, or cold, calculating men of darker days to block the wheels of their progress. With no other right than that of might, they swept away the last vestige of a once proud and powerful people, preëminent among whom, as indeed preëminent among all men of all races and of all time, stands the man to whose memory these lines are dedicated, Massasoit the Great Sachem of the Wampanoags. We have already considered the probable numerical strength of the Pokanokets and, in a general way, that of the federated tribes, calling particular attention to the Pocassets and Nausets about whom something fairly definite is known; and it is not my purpose to make further comment upon that subject except as it may be necessary to emphasize or illustrate some other matter that seems to be of sufficient importance to warrant trespassing upon the reader's patience by calling attention again and again to the situation as it was in the early days of the colonial life of New England, and particularly of the Plymouth Colony. And, in this connection, no sketch of Massasoit would be quite complete without a brief reference to the fact that in his earlier days, he had been a great war chief himself, or at least the head of a federation capable of holding its own against the tribes that were undoubtedly attempting from time to time to make inroads upon its hunting grounds; for we have it from Captain Benjamin Church, who was General Winslow's chief of staff in King Philip's war, that Annawon, Philip's great captain, after his capture, boasted of his former prowess and deeds of valor when serving under Philip's father. I use the expression, a great war chief himself or the head of a powerful federation, advisedly, for it seems to be clearly established that the Great Sachem, or Chief of Chiefs, of the Indian federations, while the head of the civil government, was not always the personal leader of his warriors in battle, that duty sometimes devolving upon some great captain who had distinguished himself by his valor, cunning and capacity for inspiring and handling large bodies of warriors. To such a captain was frequently entrusted the conduct or personal direction of the wars after a plan of campaign had been agreed upon in a council, including all the chiefs and sagamores together with the select body or class called "paniese" who were the chief men of valor. This seems particularly to have been the practice among the Five Nations of the Iroquois League, and was probably the occasional practice with the other federations, although a careful perusal of such records as are available leads to the conclusion that the Great Sachem himself in most instances personally conducted his campaigns. We do not have to look far for a reason for this. From our knowledge of Indian character, we may well infer that the Great Chiefs would be extremely reluctant to relinquish the control of their warriors to a sub-chief or captain through fear of loss of their own prestige and the acquisition of too great an ascendency on the part of their captains,

prowess on the warpath being the one qualification
that would appeal most strongly to the Indian tem-
perament and endear a chief to his people, thus
strengthening his hold upon them. Consequently
we may safely conclude that before he had been
weakened by the loss of his people through the
ravages of the pestilence of 1616–1617, and the
raids of the Tarratines upon his outlying tribes,
Massasoit was himself a noted warrior. Through
the agencies enumerated his war strength had been
reduced from three thousand or five thousand warriors, there being authority for both figures, to probably one thousand or twelve hundred, not counting
the Nipmucks, who were most likely governed as
conquered tribes, and of doubtful value in war.
That they were not of the closely allied or related
tribes, but were looked upon as inferiors, is fairly
apparent from Massasoit's remark to Roger Williams, as quoted by him in his letter to Governor
Winthrop at Boston, which will appear later. I
cannot refrain from expressing the belief that my
estimate as given above of one thousand or more is
fair; and in this connection, I will take the liberty
of digressing again from the subject of this chapter
to make another of those little side trips into territory that ought, perhaps, to have been explored
when we were inquiring into the numerical strength
of the Wampanoags, but an examination of which is
timely in connection with what I have just said,
and in the consideration of Massasoit's readiness to
treat with the colonists and the importance to them
of that friendly disposition.

At the time of Canonicus' challenge to the settlers in November, 1621, Bradford, for some reason, came to the conclusion that it was his desire to "lord it over the weaker Pokanokets and Massachusetts"; and, from what we know of that wily and ambitious chief, we may well believe that Bradford's suspicion, even if it was nothing more than that, was well founded. The Narragansetts had escaped the ravages of the pestilence, and Canonicus, taking advantage of his neighbor's weakness, had begun an offensive warfare against Massasoit, and had wrested from him the Island of Aquidnick. This probably could be accomplished only by force; but the encounter is likely to have been limited to the occupants of the island, with possibly such assistance as could be hurried to them from tribes in close proximity. The wars among the natives were undoubtedly of short duration, a single combat sometimes deciding the issue, and it might well happen that Canonicus could muster his warriors in sufficient force to conquer the island before any assistance could reach its people, and to hold it against any attempts of the weakened Wampanoags to retake it. According to the best authorities, from three to four thousand warriors stood ready to take up the War Cry of Canonicus at that time and to pass it along from village to village, like Rhoderick Dhu's summons to Clan Alpine. If he was as ambitious to extend his domain and power as some writers think, and as his attack upon the island seems to indicate, it is inconceivable that he should have refrained from further conquest if the

Wampanoags, Massachusetts and Pawtuckets, or
Pennacooks, were as weak as some writers seem to
think, Drake placing the strength of the Pawtuckets at that time at two hundred and fifty souls,
not warriors but all combined, and another writer
saying that the Massachusetts were the weakest of
all the three federations.

It is true that the Pequots at some earlier date
had subjugated the Mohicans, Niantics and other
minor tribes in Connecticut and had settled down
upon the land contiguous to that of the Narragansetts on the west; and that the bitterest hostility
existed between these two tribes or federations; but
they seem to have been at peace at this time; and
from our reading of the records of dissensions between the Pequots and the conquered tribes which
they evidently were trying to join to themselves, we
may well believe that they were then bending all
their energy to the task of consolidating the conquered territory, a task at which they were never
entirely successful. However much the Narragansetts may have feared attempts at further conquests on the part of the Pequots, there is no
evidence of any Pequot aggressions against them at
that time; and it is more than likely that the hostility of later days was first manifested by the Narragansetts themselves, being aroused in part at least
by the raid of the Pequots upon the hunting grounds
of the Niantics and the Mohicans, the former of
whom were more closely related to the Narragansetts than either of them were to the Pequots; and

the Mohicans not being held in such dread as were their conquerors.

So the fear of Pequot invasion may be eliminated as a possible deterrent to further Narragansett aggression against the Wampanoags, and we are compelled to look for another reason for Canonicus' failure to follow up his seizure of Aquidnick. There seems but one logical conclusion, and that is that the Wampanoag strength on the mainland, where the destruction of a few villages would result only in driving their occupants back upon the inland tribes by which they would be constantly augmented was sufficient to hold Canonicus in check.

These reflections lead us directly to a consideration of Massasoit's purpose in approaching the English with the olive branch of peace. Any suggestion that he did it from purely disinterested motives would be a reflection upon his sagacity. That he was running counter to the wishes of his most powerful sub-sachem, Corbitant of Pocasset, is clearly established, and it is inconceivable that he voluntarily trailed to Plymouth for the purpose of giving up something for nothing. On the other hand, he knew enough about the English not to expect something for nothing from them. The territory of his own tribes had been invaded by Harlow and Hunt, who had carried away many of his people, some to be sold into slavery, and others to be held in virtual slavery to those who desired to utilize them in further trade among the tribes. Squanto had returned, and, of course, had related his experiences; and Massasoit must have known of similar outrages perpetrated upon other tribes along the New England coast. Virginia Baker in her excellent little book, "Massasoit's Town of Sowams in Pokanoket," speaks of him as wise statesman and shrewd politician; and it is in this character that we are impelled, by a consideration of his acts, to look upon him. Squanto's account of what he had seen in England where he had spent much time and had been kindly treated must have seemed to his simple listeners like tales from the "Arabian Nights." Massasoit had heard his story and had been impressed by it; and, when he learned that voyagers from that wonderful land had settled upon his territory, he went to them, not to surrender any portion of his sovereignty, but as a king to treat with the representatives of a king. There was no thought of submission or subjection. He came to ascertain the purpose of their visit and their intentions, and when he learned that they contemplated a permanent settlement, he sat down with them to discuss terms on which they might live side by side in perfect harmony.

The memorable treaty was the outcome of this conference, and under it he accomplished his purpose as long as the men who were parties to it lived and kept a controlling hand on the affairs of the colony. It was not encroachments by Carver, Bradford, Winslow and their associates, who knew him in the early days, that caused the breach and little by little widened it until nothing short of the resort to arms could settle the differences between the two races, but the unjust suspicions, followed by the arbitrary conduct and petty acts of annoyance of a later generation. The ambitious designs of the colonists, when they had attained sufficient strength to walk alone, led them to attempt to govern the Indians as subjects, to order them about at will, to interfere in their most intimate tribal affairs, to take jurisdiction of matters that ought to have been left to tribal councils, instead of treating them as an independent and politically equal people. It was this conduct on the part of the whites that broke the chain of friendship and plunged the colonists into war with the sons of the men who had befriended them at a time when that friendship was a matter of life or death to them; a war that cost the colonists thousands of lives that might have been saved by a little tolerance and a sense of justice, and that resulted in the extermination of a once proud and powerful people.

This fatal ending of a friendship so auspiciously begun cannot justly be charged to Massasoit, nor entirely to his sons and successors. The history of the times has been written by the colonists. The Indian has left no chronicle of the events that finally impelled him to dig up the tomahawk. It is by the white man's records that both must be judged; and those records convict the colonists of a series of aggressions of sufficient seriousness to arouse the ire and stir the blood of any people who had been accustomed to range the forests and fish the streams in untrammeled freedom until the white man cunningly forged the fetters for their free born feet.

Massasoit entered into the treaty in entire good

faith, and with a fixed determination to observe it
in spirit and in letter, as is conclusively shown by
the several acts to which I shall call particular attention, by his overlooking its breach by the English in refusing to surrender Squanto, and by the
fact that the treaty was never broken by him or his
people during the forty years of his life after its
signing, nor during the short reign of his eldest son
and successor, Wamsutta, nor indeed during the
first thirteen years of the rule of his second son
Pometacom; although there were rumblings of the
approaching tempest from 1671. Indeed, the colonists tried to find evidence of bad faith on the part
of Wamsutta ten years before, but the most they
did was to establish their own bad faith in spite of
their efforts to cover it with the cloud of suspicion
against him. A further consideration of the affair
with that great chief will appear when we come to
a survey of his short term in his chieftaincy; so
I shall dismiss it for the present with the reflection
that some acts on the part of the whites during
the period which we are considering, as recorded by
themselves, are enough to raise the question whether
they were not guilty of a deliberate attempt to so
arouse and exasperate the natives, as to lead them
to acts of open hostility to be seized upon as an
excuse for exterminating the race. I am aware that
this is a serious indictment, but it is supported by
a series of aggressions that seem inexplicable on
any other theory than that they were deliberately
planned, or were perpetrated with reckless disregard
for the rights of the Indians.

Massasoit, as I have said, entered into the pact with Governor Carver in good faith. He was accustomed to dealing with men whose only bond was their word, with the simple natives, "silly savages," as Captain Smith calls them, unaccustomed to the arts of civilization and the trick of trying to find excuses for breaking their pledges, instead of studiously endeavoring to observe them, both in letter and in spirit; and he then had no reason for supposing that the English were less sincere, or that they entered into the relations defined in the pact with the intent to observe it only in so far as it served their purpose, or as long as it was useful to them. This was one of the lessons in the higher European civilization that they learned in the bitter school of experience; and the men who taught them this code of morals had no right to complain when the results of their teaching reacted upon themselves. I am reluctant to believe that Carver then looked upon his treaty in that light; but we find his immediate successor, Bradford, recording the fact that he, as early as 1622 in the episode arising out of the perfectly apparent perfidy of Squanto, was more intent upon finding an excuse for evading the treaty than upon conforming to its provisions.

So when Samoset on March 16, 1621, appeared in the street of Plymouth, and, after being entertained, departed on the next day saying he would bring Massasoit, a great Sachem who had sixty warriors under him; and apparently sent runners who had been lurking in the neighborhood, to convey to Massasoit the tidings that the English had encamped upon the hunting grounds of one of his tribes, now extinct, and had erected habitations there of a more permanent character than had ever been attempted before, the Great Sachem himself, proud ruler of more than thirty villages, with his sixty panieses, took up the trail of forty miles to visit the intruders, not for the purpose of expelling them by force, not to trade with them as had been done before along the coast, but to inquire the purpose of this unbidden camping upon the grounds of which he was still the rightful owner, even though the tribe, his tribe, that had occupied them had been wiped out. Possibly he had in mind the very thing that happened, the formation of a league with the white men, who fought with "fire and thunder," to assist him in case of further encroachments by his ambitious neighbor, Canonicus; and for which he was willing to give a full equivalent, the right to occupy the land, the assistance of his people in teaching the strangers how to compel the forest, stream and soil to yield up a subsistence, and to aid them in case of hostile attacks upon them by tribes over which he had no control, or which were likely to break away from such restraint as he had over them.

Viewed in the light of what we know, it now seems that the colonists were getting the best end of the bargain as matters then stood, and could well afford to be liberal in the construction of the duties and obligations assumed by them. True, as they increased in numbers and strength, the scale might have tipped the other way even if the treaty had been rigidly adhered to by the settlers, but this affords no excuse for its breach by them. As matters stood on that bleak day in March, 1621, with their ranks depleted by death, that had desolated nearly, if not quite, every hearth, deaths in such numbers that they dared not raise a mound to mark the spots where they had consigned their departed to earth for fear that their weakness might be discovered, they received much more than they gave. To them this friendly visit of Massasoit and his readiness to sit with them in council, to smoke with them the pipe of peace, to form with them a defensive alliance, must have seemed like a visitation of guardian angels from an unseen shore.

Words without deeds, however, are of little value, promises are easily made, and, too often, as easily broken. The shores of time are thickly strewn with the wreckage of treaties shattered by the perfidy of men who look not to their plighted word once it seems to their advantage to disregard their solemn pledges. This reflection brings us to a consideration of the benefits accruing to the colonists from the faithfulness of the natives to the pact entered into between Governor Carver and their Great Sachem.

Things moved rapidly during the first few years after the landing of the Pilgrims, and there must have been times when they were in serious doubt whether their venture was destined to success or failure. Without attempting to recite the entire history of that period, I will call attention to a few of the important events for the successful culmination of which the colonists were indebted to the Great Sachem who had pledged his friendship to them. I do this for the purpose of properly appraising the value of that friendship.

Two men occupy a unique position in the early life of the colonists. I shall have more to say about them in a later chapter, but it is not inopportune to here call attention briefly to the fact that they played an important part in assisting the settlers to establish themselves, and to enter into trade relations with the tribes; of these Squanto, it will be remembered was either the only survivor or one of the very few survivors of the Patuxets who had occupied the territory around Plymouth as far back as the hunting grounds of the Nemaskets, whose principal village was on the site now occupied by Middleboro; and consequently he was a subject of Massasoit. A brief account of his invaluable services will appear elsewhere, and my only purpose now is to suggest that without the friendship of his Great Sachem he might not have been in position to give such assistance to the colonists as to lead Corbitant, in his bitterness, to speak of him as the tongue of the English.

Hobamock, the other of these two, was one of the panieses of Massasoit, attached to his chieftaincy as counsellor and personal follower on the warpath. He came to the English shortly after the end of July, 1621, and proved to be of great help to them in extending their trade and in establishing friendly relations with the surrounding tribes. In this he was undoubtedly aided by his position as a counsellor to the Great Sachem, his influence on this account extending even beyond the hunting grounds of the Wampanoags. Besides it was he who broke away and gave the alarm that resulted in the rescue of Squanto when threatened by Corbitant. It is true that Squanto was only threatened and then let go, but what might have been his fate had not Corbitant known that Hobamock was likely to bring a hornet's nest about his ears, we can only conjecture. And so the colonists owed the continued services of Squanto to Hobamock.

Three months after Massasoit's first visit to Plymouth, as their first spring in the new world was ripening into summer, Governor Bradford, who had been elected to succeed Carver, was desirous of securing first hand information concerning the Great Sachem, how important a personage he was, and what were his surroundings, and so on July 2, 1621, Edward Winslow, who had been one of the hostages for Massasoit's safety when he entered Plymouth to confer with Governor Carver, set out accompanied by Stephen Hopkins and with Squanto as guide, to secure the desired information, to strengthen the ties of friendship, and to procure corn for planting. They arrived on July 4, and found Massasoit absent, but he soon returned and greeted them kindly. They presented him a red horseman's coat, which he donned with great pride, and a copper chain which he was to send by any messengers whom he might wish to dispatch to Plymouth, as evidence that they came from him. On this occasion they found him and his people reduced to such straits

for food that he was unable to offer them anything
to eat until the next day, when he set before his
guests two large boiled fish, which served as a repast for them and about forty of the natives. They
spent two nights in his lodge, but in such discom-
fort, as Winslow informs us in great detail, that
they arose more exhausted than when they retired.
On the third day they departed to return to Plymouth, although urged to make their visit longer
by Massasoit, who expressed regret that he had not
been able better to entertain them. Unfortunately
Winslow does not inform us what entertainment
they had after the first repast. From this and later
visits there sprung up a strong personal friendship
between Winslow and the Great Sachem which continued until the death of the former in 1655.

Hardly had this mission been successfully accomplished when there arose a great hue and cry for
one John Billington who was lost. He had gone
into the woods, and, unable to find his way out,
wandered up and down for five days, finally reaching Manomet, twenty miles down the bay. The
Manomets carried him further down the cape to
the Nausets. The governor inquired of the Indians
about him, and finally Massasoit sent word where
he was and a shallop was sent for him. The Nausets
soon after came, one hundred warriors, and "made
peace" with the colonists. It is related that of the
one hundred who came only sixty entered the village, the others holding themselves aloof. It was
at about this time that Hobamock came to live
at Plymouth. Whether he was the messenger who

brought the tidings of Billington's whereabouts and remained, or not, does not appear; but he was there in August, for it was then that the episode between him and Squanto and Corbitant, which we will have occasion to consider later, came tumbling so close on the heels of that with the Manomets and Nausets that the settlers must have been nearly distracted by the antics of their neighbors. When Captain Standish with his formidable army of fourteen men surrounded the house in which Corbitant was supposed to be holding Squanto prisoner, if indeed he had not already dispatched him, three men were "sore wounded" in getting out, and were brought to Plymouth and healed; whereupon the colonists "received the gratulations of many sachems. Yea, those of the Island of Capawack sent to make friendship, and this Corbitant himself used the mediation of Massasoit to make his peace but was shie to come near them a long while after," as the story is told by Bradford.

Following this series of events, each of which was fraught with the possibility of disaster to the settlers, came the red letter day of the whole year. On September 13, nine chiefs came to Plymouth to arrange a *modus vivendi* as modern diplomats would say; and before they got away every one of them signed an acknowledgment of allegiance to King James. Probably not one of them knew what he had done or dreamed that he had entered the town a prince, a ruler over his people, and left it a slave, for that is what the colonists tried to make of them; and their posterity have raised a great hue

and cry about the faithless Indians not submitting
to be governed by the colonists, as loyal subjects of
the same king.   Unless the rulers and holy men of
God at Plymouth loaded them with "strong water"
until they were entirely bereft of their senses, they
undoubtedly thought that they were treating on
equal terms with the settlers, signing a treaty of
alliance, and not a craven surrender of their sovereignty.   These nine chiefs were:

OHQUAMEHUD, said by Drake to be a Wampanoag, and undoubtedly true in the broad sense in
which we use the term, for the same name, though
spelled Oquomehod, appears on a deed from the
Nausets to the people of New Plymouth in 1666.

CAWNACOME, whom Drake identifies as Conecamon, Sachem of Manomet; and I desire to digress
at this point to call attention to the fact that this
latter spelling is identical with that of the name of
Epenow's companion in captivity when he was
carried away by Harlow in 1611, and undoubtedly
identifies the former victim of English cupidity
with the later sachem of his tribe.

OBBITINUA, said by Drake to be Obbatinewat,
sachem of the Massachusetts, and subject to Massasoit.   Dexter disagrees with Drake, on the theory
that the colonists would not have asked him to submit himself by reason of his relations with Massasoit.   This reasoning seems illogical to me, because
there is strong ground for believing that the Massachusetts were not subjects, but allies of Massasoit,
in fact the weight of authority strongly points to
this conclusion; besides, even if he were a subject

of Massasoit, Dexter's reasoning seems weak in view of the fact that nearly all the sachems who submitted themselves at that time were clearly subjects of Massasoit.

NATTAWAHUNT, probably Natawanute or Attawanhut of Connecticut, although Drake inclines to the belief that this is Nashacowan, a Nipmuck chief who was a subject of Massasoit. My reason for believing it to be the former is that Attawanhut, a Connecticut River sachem, had been dispossessed of his territory along the Fresh (Connecticut) River by Wapyquent, or Tattoepan as he is most frequently called, and Winslow, who had large property holdings in Connecticut and spent a considerable part of his time there, restored him to his former possessions, quite likely as a reward for his submission, and in the expectation of profiting by giving him, a subject of the king, the name of ruling the natives in the vicinity.

CAUNBITANT (Corbitant), Sachem of Pocasset whom we have already noticed.

CHICATAUBUT, of the Massachusetts.

QUADEQUINA, Massasoit's younger brother, who accompanied him to Plymouth on the occasion of his first visit and was undoubtedly one of the two "Kings of Pokanoket" whom Captain Dermer met in the wilds of Nemasket in 1619.

HUTTAMOIDEN, whom I am unable to identify from the writings of contemporary historians either by this name or any other bearing a close resemblance to it.

APPANOW, whom Drake takes to be Aspinet of

Nauset, taking issue with other early writers, who think it was Epenow of Capawack. The closer similarity in sound together with the recorded fact that after the episode of Corbitant, Squanto and Hobamock the month previous, "those (Sachems) of the island of Capawack sent to make friendship," leads me to believe that it was Epenow. He had *sent* the month before and now undoubtedly *came* in person. This is probably the same Epenow who, with Conecamon, was carried away by Harlow in 1611, and made a thrilling escape three years later, as already related.

The confusion in names resulting from changes in spelling from sound leaves us in doubt as to the identity of some of the men of that period. The names, being written down by some Englishman as the sounds struck his ear, were spelled in almost as many ways as there were men who had occasion to write them. Consequently, where differences of opinion arise concerning the identity of particular individuals, we are obliged to decide for ourselves which appears the most reasonable.

My only reason for going into this question in detail and attempting to establish the identity of these sachems is to call attention to the far reaching effects of the treaty of March 22, 1621, for there can be no question that the event of September 13 was the direct outgrowth of that treaty, as, indeed, were all the events to which I have just called attention.

There were other matters arising at a later time in which the action of the natives was unquestionably influenced by the alliance between the Wampanoags and the English; but I will content myself with calling attention briefly to one of them at this time, one that will be more fully discussed in another chapter, but is of so much consequence in connection with the subject now under consideration, that this array of the direct benefits resulting to the colonists from their treaty with Massasoit would not be complete without some reference to it; and that is the challenge sent by Canonicus to Plymouth in November, 1621, in the form of a bundle of arrows wrapped in a rattlesnake's skin. We are accustomed to think of Governor Bradford's defiant reply, accompanied by the same skin filled with powder and musket balls, as the only deterrent to Canonicus' ambitious project of attacking the colony. But it should be borne in mind that the Narragansetts could reach Plymouth only by sailing around Cape Cod, which was impracticable, or by crossing Wampanoag territory. This would be an act of open hostility to the latter unless assented to, so it may have been, not the powder and balls alone, but the knowledge that he would have to contest his way with Massasoit's warriors, as well, that held the wily Canonicus in check. The Narragansetts at that time could muster at least three thousand warriors, and if the Wampanoags had been hostile to the English or even passive, it does not require any particularly prophetic vision or power of divination to read the result to the colonists.

And so the first year passed without even the

suspicion of any lack of good faith on the part of
either the natives or the colonists; for no one ever
thought of blaming Massasoit for the acts of Corbitant, or of the Manomets and Nausets. Corbitant's Pocassets were almost or quite as strong
numerically as the Pokanokets alone, and their territory adjoined; and the Manomets and Nausets
were way down on Cape Cod. When one stops to
consider the way in which the tribes of the federation were scattered, and the natives' natural love of
freedom from interference, it is easy to see that
the Great Sachem who could hold them together at
all in times of peace must be both diplomat and
warrior.

But in the spring of 1622 Squanto, who evidently
was nourishing ambitions of his own, became jealous
of Hobamock, and caused rumors to be circulated
which cast some doubt upon the sincerity of Massasoit's friendship; and Bradford tells us that
"much anxiety existed which was increased by the
conduct of Massasoit, who seemed to frown on us,
and neither came nor sent to us as formerly." The
valuation which they placed upon his friendship at
that time, can easily be seen from this passage from
Bradford himself. Massasoit had good reason to
frown on them, and to refrain from coming or sending to them as formerly. This was after Squanto's
treachery to his Great Sachem had been discovered,
of which a more particular account will be found
in the chapter dealing with him, and Massasoit had
himself gone to Plymouth to request his delivery to
him in pursuance of the treaty and had sent messen-

gers for the same purpose, all to no avail. This might well cause him to wonder if the English looked upon the treaty as creating obligations and imposing duties upon only one of the signatories; and he may have felt himself released from a strict observance of its terms. From a remark made by him after Winslow had administered to him and relieved him of his distress in March, 1623, it is apparent that the Great Chief's distrust of the English, arising from Bradford's refusal to give Squanto up to him, was not entirely removed until that time.

That there was ground for the colonists' anxiety is apparent from the disclosure made by Massasoit after his relief by Winslow; and that there was justification for the acts of the natives we will show in a subsequent paragraph; but, after Winslow's visit to Sowams, there does not appear to have been any suspicion on the part of the settlers that Massasoit was a party to their projects, although he knew of them.

Sometime in March, 1623, word of Massasoit's illness reached Plymouth, and, at Governor Bradford's behest, Edward Winslow again set out for Sowams, accompanied by Hobamock and a "gentleman from London, named John Hamden," perhaps the John Hampden who afterwards distinguished himself as a leader of the Parliamentary forces in the struggle between the Commons and Charles II. Bradford desired them to make this trip to express to Massasoit his friendship, and to obtain a conference with Dutch traders who were reported to have been driven ashore in Narragansett Bay.

Before their arrival the ship had been gotten off and so this part of their errand came to naught. Not so the other purpose, however, for on arriving at Massasoit's lodge, they found him very ill, scarcely able to speak and wholly unable to see. When he asked who had come, and was told Winslow, he exclaimed: "Ah, Winslow, I shall never see thee again!" By administering some simple remedies and scraping off a thick coating which had gathered in his throat and on his tongue, Winslow soon relieved him of his suffering; whereupon he said: "Now I see the English are my friends and love me, and whilst I live I will never forget this kindness they have showed me." The doubt existing since the episode over Squanto, fostered by some one of his wily sub-sachems, unquestionably Corbitant, who had whispered suspicions into his ears during his sickness, was resolved; and Massasoit kept his word.

His sagamores and allies who had come to visit him, some from a distance of a hundred miles, were told how his friends, the English, had restored him to health.

When they were about to return to Plymouth, Massasoit called together his most trusted counsellors, of whom Hobamock was one, and, in the presence of all of them, directed Hobamock to acquaint Winslow with the existence of a plot against Weston's colony at Wessagusset and the settlement at Plymouth. He informed them that the Massachusetts Indians were the chief instigators of the conspiracy and implicated the natives of Nauset,

Paomet, Sokones, Mattachiest, Manomet, Agawam
and the Island of Capawack, most of whom were
his subjects, and among which were several of those
tribes whose sachems had subscribed the declaration of allegiance to King James eighteen months
before.

It is significant that all the tribes implicated were
those who lived remote from Pokanoket, and, especially, that Corbitant was not openly mixed up
in the affair. That he was in sympathy with the
conspirators there is no doubt; and that he had endeavored to secure his Great Sachem's consent to
his making common cause with them is almost as
certain; and Massasoit's withholding of that consent, notwithstanding his own serious grievance, is,
in itself, striking evidence of his exalted character.
The information given by him at that time was of
inestimable value to the colonists, as it enabled
their doughty Captain Standish to take the necessary steps to put an end to the conspiracy and save
the colonies.

The man who accepts at its par value the saying
"There is no good Indian but a dead Indian," will
see in this conspiracy conclusive evidence of Indian
treachery and faithlessness, and will say that Massasoit, knowing of it, had silently acquiesced in it up
to the time of his restoration to health by Winslow,
revealing it then only from gratitude for his recovery.
To such critics, I would call attention to the fact
that he showed his superiority to the English in his
display of gratitude, for there is no evidence of any
manifestation of appreciation of favors received in

all their dealings with the Indians unless there was attached to it the expectation of further favors; and I would also call attention to the fact that the colonists had themselves, only a few short months before, protected a traitor to Massasoit in plain violation of the express provisions of the treaty, the first breach; and all the natives undoubtedy knew of it. This act may well have caused the simple natives to look upon the treaty as abrogated; and to consider themselves released from all obligations assumed under that or any subsequent stipulations or agreements; and Massasoit had good cause to share in such feeling.

But for this illness of the Great Sachem, the timely arrival of Winslow, and the efficacy of his simple remedies to alleviate the suffering man and arrest the progress of the disease, the colonists might have perished at the hands of the conspirators, and another awful example of savage treachery been furnished to the world; and the major part of humanity would have accepted it at its face value, without looking into the first great cause. Indeed, the history of those times, as recorded by Bradford, might never have seen the light of day, and without his record, his failure to keep the faith with Massasoit might never have become known; for it is from his own narrative, providentially preserved, that we ascertain the story of the straining of the friendly relations between the whites and the natives.

One incident, perhaps better than any other recorded, except that of his disclosure to Winslow of the plot against the colonies, serves to illustrate the extent to which the old chief was influenced by gratitude for favors received and love for his friends. In 1637 Arthur Peach, a former servant of Winslow's, with three accomplices, killed a Narragansett Indian in cold blood. We shall see more of the details in the chapter devoted to Miantonomo, and for the purpose of concluding the brief mention here we will let Roger Williams tell the story. In his letter to Governor Winthrop of the Massachusetts Bay Colony, he says, "Ousamequin coming from Plymouth told me that the four men were all guilty. I answered but one; he replied true, one wounded him, but all lay in wait two days and assisted. Also that the principal must not die, for he was Mr. Winslow's man; and also that the Indian was by birth a Nipmuck man, so not worthy that any other man should die for him."

Williams had been banished from Salem two years before this and on his way to the Narragansett country, "on foot and alone in the dead of winter," he had been kindly entertained by Massasoit at Sowams; and they appear to have been on very friendly terms thereafter.

I cannot refrain, in passing, from referring to one little pleasantry of the Great Sachem at the expense of Winslow and his friends, and I will let the old chronicler tell the story. "Mr. Winslow coming in his bark from Connecticut to Narragansett, — and he left it there, — and intending to return by land, he went to Osamekin (Massasoit), the sagamore, his old ally, who offered to conduct him home to Plymouth. But before they took their journey,

Osamekin sent one of his men to Plymouth to tell them that Mr. Winslow was dead; and directed him to show how and where he was killed. Whereupon there was much fear and sorrow at Plymouth. The next day when Osamekin brought him home, they asked him why he sent such a word etc. to which he answered that it was their manner to do so, that they might be more welcome when they came home."

Perhaps the best tribute to the character of the Great Sachem extant is contained in the lamentation of Hobamock as poured into the ears of Winslow and Hamden when on their way to visit him in his sickness in 1623. He told them they would never see his like again among the Indians, continuing, "He is no liar, he was not bloody and cruel like other Indians; in anger and passion he was soon reclaimed, easy to be reconciled toward such as had offended him, ruled by reason in such measure as he would not scorn the advice of mean men; and that he governed his men better with few strokes than others did with many, truly loving where he loved; yea, he feared we had not a faithful friend left among the Indians; showing how he had oft times restrained their malice etc. continuing a long speech, with such signs of lamentation and unfeigned sorrow as would have made the hardest heart relent."

Such was the tribute of one of his counsellors and men of valor, who had lived with him and under his rule, who had sat with him in council and followed him on the warpath.

Carver, Bradford, Winslow, Brewster, Standish, in fact all the men who played a leading part in the opening scene of the drama enacted upon the bleak New England coast, passed from the stage of human action, leaving the old chief still directing the affairs of his federation; but finally, he too laid down the sceptre and was gathered to his fathers in whose faith he died, having refused to accept the white man's religion, though undoubtedly hearing it preached from time to time. Whether his own inherent honesty revolted at the practices of the men who professed a higher religion, we do not know; and whether, in his declining years he read in the encroachments of the men he had befriended, the approaching doom of his own people is wholly a matter of conjecture. The exact date of his departure from earth to the land of Ponemah is not recorded, nor does any one know where his remains were buried.* Drake says he was alive as late as September, 1661, but a deed given by Wamsutta dated April 8, 1661, conveying what is now the town of Attleboro, begins "Know All Men by These Presents that I, Wamsutta, alias Alexander, Chief Sachem of Pokanoket." This leaves some doubt concerning the accuracy of Drake's conclusion, although, like Passaconaway, Massasoit may have surrendered the tomahawk of authority to his eldest son before his death.

Gone were the white men who knew him in his prime, when he governed his people "better with few strokes than others with many," when he "re-

* See note at end of chapter.

strained their malice," and stood the uncompromising friend of the English, refusing to listen to the appeals of his sub-chiefs to speak the word which would have kindled a holocaust for the settlers. Gone were the friends of his early days, who valued his friendship and loved him for his native honesty and sincerity. In their place had arisen another generation, interested in him and his people only as the possessors of land they coveted; and so far as we know not a white man dropped a tear over the cold form of the hero who had so often stood between them and destruction.

Of him General Fessenden well says, "This Chief has never had full justice done to his character": and I have not attempted anything like a complete biography. Of his early life nothing is known except the glimpses revealed by the lamentation of Hobamock and the boasting of Annawon; and even subsequent to that time, there are so many voids, so much that is left to be inferrred from the writings of contemporary historians that the task is well nigh impossible. My only purpose has been to call attention to the qualities he possessed in such a way that "full justice may be done to his character." So little is really known of his early life that historians have not been able even to tell us his name, that is, the name bestowed upon him at birth. Massasoit and Ousamequin are the two names handed down to us by the early writers; and each of these has a multitude of variations. "Massasoyt" is the way Bradford has it in his first mention of him, and undoubtedly fairly represents the sound as he heard it from Samoset; and Prince says, "the ancient people from their fathers in Plymouth pronounce it Mas-sa-so-it."

Bicknell tells us that his true or tribal name was Ousamequin, made up of ousa, yellow, and mequin, feather, and that Massasoit means Great Sachem. Others, Peirce among them, think that he changed his name from Massasoit to Ousamequin in 1632, when he was at war with the Narragansetts; while still others believe he adopted the latter name on the death of his brother Quadequina. He does not appear to have been known to the Pilgrims by this name until long after his first appearance among them, but this really signifies nothing, as it may well be that they were in ignorance of his true name for a long time, calling him by that which they heard from the lips of Samoset; and that worthy may have used his title and not his name in speaking of him. So there is no real conflict between Prince and Bicknell, and color is lent to the claim of the latter by the well known practice among the Indians of naming their children for some tangible object, either animate or inanimate, hence Yellow Feather.

Whatever his mother may have called him, to whatever name he may have responded when pronounced by a fond father or by brothers and sisters, Massasoit he is to history, and Great Sachem he was in name and in fact; and as Massasoit his memory should be kept green, and his services to the colonists, as recorded by them, perpetuated for the generations yet to come; generations who will draw inspiration and new courage and zeal in the cause of freedom and humanity from the story of perils encountered, and hardships endured and overcome by the fathers, with the assistance of the friendly natives under Massasoit, in establishing upon these shores a haven of civil and religious liberty, "an asylum for the oppressed of all nations."

It is to Massasoit that we pay our tribute of respect and admiration for the manly virtues, the heroic qualities, that have endeared him to every true American who has taken the pains to analyze properly the records and acquaint himself with the facts that go to make up the beginning of American history.

NOTE.— I am indebted to Miss Virginia Baker of Warren, R. "Ancient Lowams" for the information that a few years ago an Indian burial place was excavated in that town, and in one of the graves were found a feather war bonnet, the remains of two fine muskets and a roll of gold lace. All these things indicate the burial place of a man of high rank; and the known fact that the red horseman's coat presented to Massasoit by Winslow was trimmed with gold lace, leads to the inquiry whether this was the grave of that great chief.

VI

MASSASOIT'S FAMILY

WHILE nothing definite is known of Massasoit's ancestry, the fact that the Great Chieftaincy of the federation passed from him to his eldest son and then from the latter to a younger brother, together with what we know of the hereditary character of the position among the other Algonquin groups and tribes, establishes beyond question his connection with a line of kings. Whether his father occupied the position before him, or it was handed down collaterally, does not definitely appear, nor is it of any special interest, except as it might throw some light upon the customs and laws of descent of this particular federation, and as matter of genealogical research, which possesses a fascination for most men. Who the man is and whence he came are always questions that arouse our interest in connection with those who have occupied prominent positions in the affairs of nations, not so much that it matters, for it is the man that counts, but that we sometimes like to speculate upon the conditions which have contributed to the production of the character which leaves its impress upon the history of the times.

At the beginning of the white man's history in New England, Massasoit was known to have had two brothers living. Whether there were other brothers or sisters does not appear. Of the two brothers mentioned in history, QUADEQUINA accompanied him to Plymouth in March, 1621, and is described as "a very proper, tall young man of a very modest and seemly countenance." He is generally credited with being one of the two "Kings of Pokanoket" whom Captain Dermer interviewed at Nemasket in June, 1619, this conclusion undoubtedly being drawn from the fact that he appears to have been Massasoit's companion at and after the time of his first actual introduction to history. He was probably next in age to Massasoit, as the other brother does not appear to have been particularly noticed until a much later date.

The part played by him in the affairs of the tribe or federation and in their dealings with their neighbors and the whites seems to have been an inconsequential one, which leads to the conclusion that he was simply a younger brother of the "King," and, in consequence of his royal blood, a close counsellor and frequent companion. He died within a few years of the landing of the Pilgrims.

The second brother of the Great Sachem whose name is variously written, as AKKOMPOIN, Uncompawen, Woonkaponehunt, and Vucumpowet, does not appear prominently in history until King Philip's war, in which he was one of that Great Sachem's chief counsellors and war captains, although his name appears with that of Philip on an agreement made with the Plymouth authorities on August 6, 1662, where it is written under that of "Philip, Sachem of Pokanoket," as "Vucumpowet, unkell to the above said Sachem." As I shall not have occasion to refer to him again, a word concerning his position in the Chiefs' Council will not be out of place here. That he was an active participant in the affairs of the federation during Philip's reign is apparent from the fact that in addition to the treaty or agreement of August 6, 1662, he also signed with Philip two others, one at Taunton, April 10, 1671, and the other at Plymouth, September 9, 1671. He is known to have been with Philip as counsellor and captain in the war that bears the name of the latter; and, in this capacity, he accompanied Philip on an expedition started against Plymouth in July, 1676. This project proving not feasible, the party turned back at Bridgewater, and having felled a tree across a river in the line of their march, to be used as a bridge, Akkompoin, who was one of the last to attempt to cross, was shot by the English who came up before he got away. This was on July 31, 1676, and it was this same bridge upon which Philip was seen sitting the next day, but escaped.

The known children of Massasoit were Wamsutta, Pometacom or Metacomet, Sunconewhew, Amie, and possibly another daughter, as Philip had a sister who was captured on the same day that her uncle Akkompoin was shot, who may have been Amie, although Peirce says there is no reason to suppose it was she, and as she married Tuspaquin

who had a wife living in September, 1676, there is
very good reason for supposing that the one captured in July was not Amie.

WAMSUTTA was first known as Mooanam, and
both he and his younger brother Pometacom were
given English names at the request of their father
who brought them to Plymouth, apparently for that
purpose, Wamsutta being then named Alexander
and Pometacom, Philip, for Alexander the Great of
Macedon and his father Philip, respectively. Wamsutta succeeded his father upon the death of the
latter or possibly before. I have already called attention to the fact that he signed himself "Chief
Sachem of the Pokanokets" some months before the
last date at which some writers assert that Massasoit was still alive. This may be explained on the
theory that the aged chief turned over the affairs
of the federation to his son in his old age. Before
he assumed the active management of the tribal
affairs, he seems to have participated with his
father in the sales of land and the making of treaties,
whether in pursuit of some arrangement between
themselves by which Wamsutta became associated
in the government, or at the insistence of the English to guard against future contingencies, we do
not know. At any rate, we find the deed of Pokanoket given in 1653 signed by both, to say nothing
of the renewal in 1639 of the original league of Massasoit and Carver, or of Roger Williams' declaration that when he first came to the Narragansett
country, in 1636, Massasoit and Mooanam, his son,
gave him Seekonk, which the Plymouth colony

claimed under their grant from the authorities in England, who, of course, had no title to it.

In 1662, the government at Plymouth became suspicious of Wamsutta, and sent Captain Thomas Willett to investigate the truth of rumors that had reached them to the effect that the sachem was attempting to secure the coöperation of the Narragansetts in a revolt which he was planning against the whites. Willett was told by Wamsutta that the whole story was a fabrication of the Narragansetts to injure him and his people with the English. He agreed to attend the next session of the Court at Plymouth, but did not put in an appearance. The colonists afterwards concluded from some rumors that came to them that he was on a visit to the Narragansett country, and this added to their suspicions, they apparently assuming the authority to say when and where he should move, and never giving him or any of his race credit for visiting another friendly tribe for any other purpose than to stir up trouble for them. The government then sent Major Winslow, the commandant of the colonial militia, to bring him to Plymouth, just as though he was a common criminal, and they had jurisdiction over him.

Like his father before him and his brother who followed him in the great chieftaincy, Wamsutta had hunting camps at various places in what remained of his domain. There is known to have been one in what is now Raynham, one at Titicut, and one on the shore of Munponset Pond in Halifax. It was at the latter that Major Winslow found him with a number of his warriors at breakfast with their guns outside. Of the three early writers who relate this incident, two say he had eighty men with him, and the other says eight. Although apprised of the approach of the English, he made no attempt to secure his arms or to escape, but remained quietly at his repast, which ought to have 'been enough to disarm the suspicion of any but an evil-minded man looking for trouble; but not Winslow. He took the guns and, entering the lodge, demanded that Wamsutta go with him to Plymouth, a virtual prisoner, to answer to nothing, to men who had no authority over him. He refused, whereupon Winslow, pursuing the usual high-handed methods of the day, presented a loaded pistol to his breast threatening him with instant death if he persisted in his refusal. After a parley with his people, he submitted, and they took up the journey, his family accompanying him. He was offered a horse, but declined, saying if the women and children could walk, he could. The party spent the night at Major Winslow's house in Duxbury, where Wamsutta was stricken with a raging fever, brought on, no doubt, by the outrages that the whites had perpetrated upon him. He was not their subject, but was the proud ruler of an independent people, and his spirit was broken by the inhumanity of the men who could not have secured a foothold upon the soil without the protection afforded them by his father. Thus are the honest mistakes of men visited upon their children.

Wamsutta's people begged to be allowed to take him to his home, which the English in their magnanimity permitted on condition that they would return him to Plymouth when he had recovered. He was called to a Higher Tribunal, however, and let us hope a more just and merciful one, for he died while descending a river in his canoe. Thus passed the eldest son of the defender of the colonies, and thus began King Philip's war by the invasion of Wampanoag territory by armed men, and the capture of the king of the country at the point of a loaded pistol; and yet, there are men even now, who tell us that King Philip started the trouble.

Wamsutta married Tatapanum, otherwise called WEETAMO, and known to history as the "Squaw Sachem of the Pocassets." She is believed to have been the daughter of Corbitant; and in the war which resulted from the series of outrages of which the arrest and moral murder of her husband was the culmination, she followed the fortunes of her brother-in-law Philip, twice her brother-in-law in fact, for Philip married her sister, Wootonekanuske. She was a widow when Wamsutta married her, and, after his death, she married a third husband about whom nothing is known except his name, Quequequanchett. She subsequently married a fourth, Petononowit, whom she left in consequence of his having espoused the English cause; and she then formed a liaison with a young Narragansett Sachem, Quinapen, one of Philip's captains. She was drowned by the breaking up of a raft near Mettapoisett in August, 1676. Word had reached her that the English forces were approaching, and there being no canoes available, she attempted to escape

on an improvised raft which was not strong enough
to withstand the buffeting of the seas. Her body
was recovered by the English who humanely cut off
her head and exposed it on a pole at Taunton,
where, as one of their eminent divines scoffingly
informs us, it was seen by some of her people who
had been taken prisoner, who set up a lamentation
saying it "was the head of their queen." Little
did the poor mourners know the fate that was in
store for them, or they might have raised a prayer
to the Great Spirit to be allowed to share in that
of their "Queen." Slavery, worse than death, "the
store of rods for free born backs and stocks for free
born feet," was the lot reserved for them by their
Christian captors.

No doubt the apologists for the colonists will say
that Weetamo should not have joined in Philip's
nefarious scheme. She had seen her people robbed
of their inheritance, their means of securing a livelihood taken away under the pretence of purchase,
her husband, with nothing proved against him,
dying at the hands of the men whose existence had
depended upon the friendship of his father, as truly
as though he had been given the deadly poison
which his people always believed was administered
to him; but in spite of all this, she should have
kissed the hand that smote her.

POMETACOM, Massasoit's second son and Wamsutta's successor when the latter died in 1662,
played such an important part in the affairs between
the Indians and their oppressors that a separate
chapter will be devoted to him and his captains.

SUNCONEWHEW was the third son of Massasoit. But little is known of him, his name appearing but once of which I find any mention in connection with the so-called sale of lands to the English, and that with Philip's on a deed confirming the sale of Rehoboth by Massasoit in 1641, the confirmatory deed bearing date March 30, 1668. It is said that Philip had a brother killed July 18, 1775, who was a great captain and had been educated at Harvard College. As there is no record of any other sons of Massasoit except these three, this was undoubtedly Sunconewhew.

AMIE, the only daughter of Massasoit of whom anything definite is known, married Tuspaquin of Assawamsett, commonly called the "Black Sachem." Their oldest son, William Tuspaquin, followed his father in fighting for his people in King Philip's war, in the early part of which he met his death. Their second son is said to have been a noted warrior, and to have had a part of his jaw bone shot away in battle. We are left in doubt concerning the part he played in the war, whether he was fighting with his own people or with the English. He is mentioned as a member of Captain James Church's company; and it is reported that he died suddenly after the war while sitting in his wigwam. These two statements, however, are not entirely irreconcilable with the supposition that he may have been faithful to his own people, as he might have joined Captain Church's company after the war; although how he and his family escaped slavery is almost beyond comprehension; or how he came to die suddenly while sitting in his wigwam; for while the men of note, the chiefs and sons of chiefs who followed Philip, died suddenly, it was not while sitting in their wigwams.

There is one fact that lends color to the theory that he followed the fortunes of his Great Chief as did his father and elder brother, and that is the indignation of some of his children when their brother, Benjamin Tuspaquin, second, married Assawetough, or Mercy Felix, the daughter of John Sassamon, whom they regarded as a traitor to his people.

The only known descendants of Massasoit now living trace their lineage through this son of his daughter, Amie.

In 1917, the General Court of Massachusetts passed the following:

"RESOLVE GRANTING ANNUITIES TO TEEWE-LEEMA MITCHELL AND HER TWO SISTERS, OF THE WAMPANOAG TRIBE OF INDIANS.

Resolved, That there shall be paid annually from the treasury of the commonwealth, in equal quarterly installments from the first day of December, nineteen hundred and sixteen, the sum of one hundred dollars each to Teeweleema Mitchell, Wootonekanuske Mitchell, and Zeriah Robinson, three sisters, aged and needy Indian women of the Wampanoag tribe, residents of Lakeville, who are descendants of King Philip's sister, and descendants of Massasoit. (Approved February 21, 1917.)"

General Ebenezer W. Peirce in his "Indian History, Biography and Genealogy" traces the descent of these three women from Benjamin Tuspaquin, giving names in each successive generation, and mentioning another sister, Emma J., who married Jacob C. Safford and had two children living at the time of the writing of his book in 1878. I am recently in receipt of a communication from Charlotte L. Mitchell, the Wootonekanuske named in the resolve quoted above, in answer to an inquiry, in which she writes that one of these children, Helen G. Safford is still living, but is confined in a hospital for the insane. She also speaks of her own brother Alonzo as still living, unmarried and in feeble health. Of the three annuitants above named, Zerviah Robinson was born (Mitchell) June 17, 1828, Teeweleema (known as Melinda) April 11, 1836, and Wootonekanuske (known as Charlotte L.), my correspondent, November 2, 1848.

So if these five are all the living descendants of Massasoit, as Peirce asserts, the royal line will become extinct in the next generation.

In 1917, the General Court of Massachusetts also passed the following:

"RESOLVE TO AUTHORIZE THE PAYMENT OF AN ANNUITY TO FANNIE S. BUTLER THROUGH THE MAYOR OF THE CITY OF BOSTON.

Resolved, That there be allowed and paid out of the treasury of the Commonwealth to the mayor of the city of Boston an annuity of two hundred and fifty dollars, to be expended by the mayor for the benefit of Fannie S. Butler, granddaughter of the late Sylvia Sepit Thomas and daughter of the late Mary Angeline Thomas Butler, members of the Wampanoag tribe of Indians, for the rest of her natural life, beginning with the first day of December in the year nineteen hundred and sixteen, and payable in equal quarterly instalments.

Chapter one hundred and seventeen of the resolves of the year nineteen hundred and fourteen is hereby repealed. (Approved February 17, 1917.)"

This was an increase in an annuity first granted in 1914, at which time the press spoke of the annuitant as a descendant of Massasoit, and the last of the Wampanoags. That she is a descendant of Massasoit is contrary to the conclusion of Peirce, and evidently was not satisfactorily established before the Committee of the Legislature which considered the matter, otherwise they would have been likely to set out that fact, as they did in the case of the Mitchell family. Miss Mitchell, in her letter to me, says that Fannie S. Butler is not of the family. That she is not, as was stated in the newspapers of that day, the last of the Wampanoags, is conclusively shown.

My correspondent may, however, have followed the same family traditions that guided Peirce in his writings, which fail to take account of the possibility of other branches of the Benjamin Tuspaquin

family. This writer took great pains to trace the
descent of this particular branch, but appears to
have been content to establish their lineage and
rest there. He names the four children of Benjamin, as Esther, Hannah, Mary and Benjamin
second.

Esther married Tobias Sampson, a "praying Indian" who lived on the reservation set off by resolve of the General Court of Massachusetts in
1701, and is said to have died without issue. There
was an Esther Sampson living on the reservation in
1764, but whether the same or another of the same
name is not clear, although there is some reason for
believing that it was not Benjamin's daughter.

Hannah married and had two children, neither of
whom married.

Mary married Isaac Sissel and had three children, Mary, Mercy and Arabella. The family tradition says that two of them died in infancy; but
in 1764, Mary and Mercy were on the reservation.
This leaves only Arabella unaccounted for; and it
is so easy to drop a link in the attempts to pass
such matters down from generation to generation
that it may well be that there were two children of
Isaac and Mary Sissel who died in infancy, besides
these three; and that Arabella, like Mary and
Mercy, may have lived to womanhood, but unlike
them, she may have married and left progeny who,
through the long lapse of time and by reason of the
remoteness of the relationship, may have been lost
sight of by those who attempt to hand down traditions without complete records.

Benjamin second, as I have at least suggested if not plainly stated, married Assawetough, a daughter of John Sassamon, the Indian alleged to have been murdered for disclosing to the whites King Philip's plan for a general uprising among the Indians; and who, according to tradition, was the same man who had given to him for his services in the Pequot war, and as his share of the spoils of that war, a "young little squaw," whom he afterwards married and who is said to be a daughter of Sassacus. If the family tradition which connects John Sassamon with the Massachusetts Indian of a somewhat similar name who served with the English in the war against Sassacus is reliable, it will be seen that this "young little squaw" became the mother of Assawetough or Mercy Felix, as she appears in history and tradition; and that their great grandchildren, the Mitchell family of Lakeville, are descended in the direct line, not only from Massasoit, but also from Sassacus, the Pequot Chief; for Benjamin and Mercy had one daughter, named Lydia, who married an Indian named Walmsley and had five children.

Four of these do not appear in the pages of any known history, biography or genealogy; nor do any public records, so far as known, indicate what became of them. Whether they married and have descendants living is not definitely known, notwithstanding the "family tradition."

The fifth, Paul, had seven children, four of whom are not mentioned beyond their names; two of whom are mentioned by Peirce as having married,

and are left there; and the other, Phebe, was the
mother of the annuitants named in the first of the
resolves quoted above. The records of those early
days were not as complete as those of today; and
it may well be that some of these whom I have mentioned have handed down the blood of the Great
Sachem, the "friend of white men," to succeeding
generations.

In 1701, the General Court of Massachusetts set
aside a tract of land in what was then Freetown
but is now a part of Fall River, as a reservation for
the friendly Indians, and of the twenty-five lots
into which this reservation was divided, four, numbered 19, 20, 21, and 22, were assigned to the lineal
descendants of Benjamin Tuspaquin. At the first
survey of these lots in 1707, Isaac Sissel received as
his share lot No. 20. In 1764, on the second survey, this lot was in possession of his daughters,
Mercy and Mary. At this second survey, lot No.
19 was found to be in possession of "Sarah Squin
and Esther Sampson," said to be grandchildren of
Benjamin Squamnaway.

The ease with which Tuspaquin could be con-
tracted to Squin, together with the fact that these
two women were occupying a lot assigned to the
descendants of Tuspaquin, leads to the conclusion
that Benjamin Squamnaway was Benjamin Tuspaquin. The only Esther Sampson mentioned in
history in connection with the descendants of Massasoit, outside of this reference, was the daughter of
Benjamin Tuspaquin, and she died childless. It is
possible, of course, that the Esther Sampson who

was on that lot in 1764 was Benjamin Tuspaquin's daughter and not his granddaughter; but this is extremely doubtful, for in that case she would be the sister of Benjamin Tuspaquin second who married the daughter of John Sassamon and the young little squaw whom he had given to him at the conclusion of the Pequot war, one hundred and twenty-seven years before, and Sassamon had been dead ninety years at the time of this second survey of the lots.

However it may be, there is a numerous family in Fall River and vicinity who, through an old family tradition, claim descent from the Esther Sampson who resided on the reservation in 1764. If this tradition is well founded, and if "Sarah Squin and Esther Sampson" were granddaughters of Benjamin Tuspaquin, it will be readily seen that this family of which I write are lineal descendants of Massasoit. To all appearances they are pure whites, although there is another strain of Indian blood running through the family besides the one I have mentioned.

I speak of this matter, not for the purpose of establishing the claim of any particular persons to the honor of the royal blood of the house of Massasoit, as it will be noticed that I have carefully refrained from any mention of names; but to call attention to the ease with which a people may be lost in so far as its original identity is concerned, and yet may live on and on through the intermingling of its blood with that of other races, with the result that after a few generations all direct trace of it is

lost by reason of the incompleteness of the early
records. So it may well be that the blood of Massasoit and other noted warriors and chiefs of the
early days flows in the veins of men who are themselves ignorant of the fact.

VII

SAMOSET, SQUANTO AND HOBAMOCK

IT is doubtful if more welcome words of greeting ever fell on mortal ears than those that broke the startled air of Leyden Street in Plymouth on the sixteenth day of March, 1621, when the little group of weary Pilgrims gathered there heard from the lips of Samoset those words which have gone ringing down the ages as the greeting of the new world to the voyagers from the old. They had crossed a storm-swept sea, had been attacked by the natives at Nauset, and finally had effected a landing at Plymouth, the "Plimoth on Captain John Smith's map." Here they had endured the hardships of a severe New England winter, and had suffered from the ravages of disease which had greatly reduced their numbers. They had not been molested by the Indians, although in the early spring they had seen some of them prowling about the settlement, and on one occasion, some tools had been stolen while the workmen were at dinner. An air of uncertainty pervaded the place, and the appearance of the natives must have recalled with some misgiving the reception accorded them at Nauset. They had no reason to expect any different greeting here, and the "Welcome, Englishmen" from the lips of Samoset must have sounded like the "benediction that follows after the prayer."

SAMOSET told them he was not of these parts, but from Moratiggon, "eastward a day's sail with a great wind, and five days by land." He also told them that the name of the place where they had landed was Patuxet, and that the people who had occupied it had been swept away by a pestilence four years before. He told them about Squanto, a native of the place, who had been carried away across the water and could speak English, and about a Great Sachem "Massasoyte," or "the Massasoits," as one writer puts it, who lived to the west, and had sixty warriors under him. After partaking of their hospitality for the night, he went away saying he would bring Massasoit. That he did not go to Sowams, forty miles distant, is certain, for he appeared again the same day, and Massasoit did not come to Plymouth until the twenty-second. It is probable that the Indians who had been seen about the place were Nemaskets, a tribe occupying the territory around what is now Middleboro, and subject to Massasoit, or possibly Massachusetts Indians; and that some of these, at Samoset's suggestion, conveyed the intelligence to Sowams, Massasoit's village, that the English had encamped upon the hunting grounds of his extinct tribe. When Samoset returned on the seventeenth, he brought five others with him, and they returned all the tools that had been stolen.

Samoset plays but little part in the history of the colony from that time, but his name is a household word in New England to this day, and his message to the worn and weary Pilgrims is one of the great outstanding incidents in the early settlement which will be taught to our children as long as American history cherishes the tradition of the men who laid its foundations.

He was a sagamore of "Moratiggon" (Monhegan, off the coast of Maine), closely associated with the Pemaquids, if not of them; and he told the Plymouth settlers of the fishing there and conducted their fishing boats to the grounds. He had picked up a little English from the crews of ships that had been there to fish. What errand or mission brought him to the territory of the Wampanoags in that early spring of 1621 will never be definitely known; but his casual presence at that time renders his name coëval with our history, and gives him a lasting place in the annals of New England. Of his subsequent life little is known except that historians have connected him prominently with the territory around Pemaquid, Maine, and identify him with Captain John Somerset, who signed a deed of land in that vicinity on July 15, 1625.

SQUANTO, whom Samoset mentioned as one who had been to England, and could speak English better than he could, was a Patuxet. His name is given as Tisquantum by many early writers, and that is probably his true name, it being shortened by the English to that by which he is known. As we have already seen, he was one of the twenty-seven natives whom Captain Thomas Hunt had carried away and sold into slavery in 1614. After his release he had been taken to England where he had lived for some time with a man named Slaine, and had apparently been kindly treated, probably with a view to utilizing his knowledge of the New World in future trading expeditions.   He had learned some English, and came back to this country with Captain Thomas Dermer either in 1619 or on an earlier voyage. Some writers say that upon his return he became a great chief, but, if this is true, it must have been prior to 1617, as his tribe was destroyed by the plague in that year.   He was interpreter for Captain Dermer when the latter met two "Kings of Pokanoket" at "Nummastaquit" (Nemasket). Mourt, in his *Relations*, speaks of him as "the only native of Patuxet where we now inhabit," but Bradford says, "He was a native of this place and scarce any left alive besides him selfe."   The latter statement is undoubtedly the correct one, as the same writer, in speaking of an episode that occurred the following year, mentions members of his family. There is no doubt that he acted as interpreter between Governor Carver and Massasoit at the memorable first interview of the Great Sachem with the Governor, and, from that time until his death, he was of invaluable service to the English.

Perhaps the best estimate of the value of his services may be made by a consideration of what Bradford says about the matter: "He directed them how to set their corne, wher to take fish, and to procure other commodities, was also a pilott to bring them to unknown places for their profitt, and never left them till he dyed."   On another occasion he wrote: "He showed them both the maner how to set it (corn) and after how to dress and tend it. Also he tould them except they gott fish and set with it (in these old grounds) it would come to nothing, and he showed them that in the middle of April they should have store enough come up the brooke, by which they begane to build, and taught them how to take it." Winslow, too, adds a word along the same line. He says: "We set some twentie acres of corn and sowed some six acres of barley and pease, and according to the manner of the Indians, we manured our ground with Herings or rather Shadds, which we have in great abundance and take with great ease at our doores." Captain John Smith had previously alluded to the Indian method of fertilizing their corn, saying, "they stick at every plant of corne, a herring or two; which cometh in that season in such abundance, they may take more than they know what to doe with." Squanto continued with the English from the time of his first introduction to them by Samoset, adopted their religion, and died of a sudden sickness accompanied with bleeding at the nose, a common malady among the natives, while on a trading expedition to Cape Cod with Governor Bradford in September, 1622.

The value of his services is almost beyond estimate, and they appear to have been appreciated at their full worth by the early settlers. Like the rest of his race, he seems to have been ambitious and jealous, his jealousy manifesting itself principally towards Hobamock; and his ambitious designs were believed by the authorities to embrace the establishment of a powerful federation of Indians with himself at its head. Some further reference will be made to these traits of his character in connection with his relations with Hobamock, another early friend and constant assistant to the English in their hunting, fishing and trading expeditions.

HOBAMOCK has, by his own statement, given us a very definite idea of his position in his tribe. In his defence of Massasoit in 1622, he said he was a "paniese," that is one of Massasoit's "chiefest champions or men of valor." He was not only a Wampanoag, but a Pokanoket, a member of the ruling tribe in the federation, and of the Great Sachem's council. He was among those who gathered at his bedside when he was thought to be dying in March, 1623, and the one whom Massasoit, in the presence of all his counsellors, charged to tell Winslow about the plot against the whites. He came to Plymouth shortly after the episode of the lost John Billington, as already related, and may have been the messenger sent by Massasoit to tell the settlers where Billington was. He had not been long with them when he showed his fidelity to his Great Chief and to the men whom he had befriended. In August, 1621, scarcely a month after he came to the English, Corbitant of Pocasset, who appears to have been a mischief maker, waylaid him and Squanto in a house at Nemasket, and threatened them, as Bradford says, "for no other cause than that they were friendly to the English and serviceable to them." Hobamock succeeded in making his escape and hastened to Plymouth, a distance of fifteen or sixteen miles. Here he told the governor of Squanto's plight and a force of fourteen men was sent to rescue Squanto if he was alive, or to punish Corbitant, if he had been killed. On arriving at the house where they had been captured, the whites surrounded it, but soon learned that Squanto was alive, having been threatened only, and that Corbitant had gone away in the night, probably through fear of the consequences that were likely to follow his attempt to remove or, at least, to frighten the men who were of so much service to the English, once the knowledge of his scheme became known to the latter, as he well knew it would be from the moment that Hobamock broke away from him.

Thus we see that Hobamock's first notable service to the settlers was in saving to them "their tongue," as Corbitant called Squanto, and in doing this he also saved the life of the man who soon after began his plottings, not only against the one who had saved him, but also apparently against the Great Sachem of both of them. Hobamock was probably as much concerned in doing what he believed would be the will of his chief in this matter, as in saving Squanto or aiding the English, for knowing of Massasoit's friendship for them, he undoubtedly felt that he would not countenance this outrage against their friend and helper. Besides, there is good reason for believing that Corbitant was an ambitious chief and if a favorable opportunity arose for displacing Massasoit as the head of the federation without danger of a miscarriage of his schemes, he would not put it aside. In any

attempt of this sort, he would have to reckon with
the English, and so they must first be rendered
powerless. Whatever may have been Hobamock's
motives, his act resulted in much good to the colonists.

Hobamock remained with them through the winter and in the spring when they were fitting out their
shallop to go to Massachusetts Bay to trade with
the Indians there, in accordance with an assurance
they had previously given them to do so, "Hobamock told them of rumors he had that they (the
Massachusetts) were joined with the Narragansetts
and might betray them if they were not careful."
He also gave them a hint of some jealousy manifested
by Squanto towards him, which he had gathered
from whisperings between the former and other
Indians. That his suspicions of Squanto in this
direction were well founded was soon demonstrated,
for, notwithstanding the misgivings aroused by these
rumors, they sent the shallop away with both
Squanto and Hobamock on board, deeming it best
to send them both along on account of this jealousy.
They had hardly got under way when an Indian of
Squanto's family, as Bradford says, came running in,
"in seeming great fear," and told them that the
Narragansetts and, he thought, Massasoit were coming against them, and he got away to tell them, not
without danger. He said there was a gathering at
Nemasket and that he had received a blow for speaking for the English, and his face was wounded. He
told them the Indians were determined to take
advantage of Captain Standish's absence on the

trading expedition to assault the town. The governor called the men to arms and fired a gun to recall the shallop. They had not got beyond reach of the signal and returned, but no Indians appeared.

It was on this occasion that Hobamock protested his confidence in Massasoit, saying "flatly that it was false" and that he "presumed he would never have undertaken any such act without his privity, it being the manner amongst them not to undertake such enterprises without the advice and furtherance of men of his rank. The governor replied that he should be sorry that any cause of war should arise with any of the savages, but especially Massasowat, not that he feared him more than the rest, but that his love more exceeded toward him than any." Hobamock replied, "there was no cause for distrust and therefore he should do well to continue his affections." I have quoted freely from Winslow's account of this episode because it illustrates Squanto's plotting and Hobamock's confidence in his chief in the manner of one who saw the entire proceeding. That Hobamock's faith was justified soon appeared. The governor caused him to send his wife to Sowams privately to see what she could learn of the situation, "pretending other occasion, but nothing was found and all was quiet," as Bradford relates. This woman finding no indication of anything unusual among the Pokanokets told Massasoit of Squanto's accusations. Naturally, "Massasoit took offence and came to Plymouth to clear himself and showed his anger towards Tisquantum." After his return to his own village he sent a messenger to

Governor Bradford, "entreating him to give way to the death of Tisquantum who had so much abused him." Bradford was reluctant to lose the services of so valuable a man, and urged his usefulness as an interpreter, but Massasoit remained obdurate, and demanded Squanto as a "subject whom the governor could not retain without violating the treaty." He also offered many beaver skins for Bradford's consent, the messengers saying, "their Sachem had sent his own knife and them therewith to cut off his head and hands and bring them to him."

The governor sent for Squanto, who, on being confronted with the accusation against him, charged Hobamock with being the cause of his overthrow; but said he would abide by the governor's decision although he knew what his fate would be if returned to Massasoit. Winslow says the governor was about to give him up when a boat appeared at sea, and being fearful of the French, he told the Indians, "he would first know what boat that was ere he would deliver him into their custody (not knowing whether there was a combination of French and Indians). Mad with rage and impatient at delay the messengers departed in great heat." This is Winslow's account, and to us, looking at it after the lapse of three hundred years, the "great heat" causes no surprise. The Indians were not so silly as not to see through the subterfuge, and to read Bradford's determination to use every excuse and employ every pretended reason that presented itself for not complying with the terms

of the treaty, when it was to his disadvantage to
live up to its obligations.

The demand was not renewed, and Squanto was
saved, but a marked coolness on the part of Massasoit soon manifested itself and caused the settlers
some uneasiness. As I have already suggested, the
offence of Squanto, although committed in the territory over which the colonists had jurisdiction, was
against his own Great Sachem. He was a subject
of Massasoit. The only jurisdiction the English
had over him was to punish acts against themselves.
By Carver's pact he should have been delivered to
his own people to be dealt with by them according
to their own customs in such cases. Bradford recog-
nizes this fact, and makes no attempt to justify his
refusal; and Winslow tells us the governor was
about to give him up when a boat appeared in the
harbor, and Bradford seized upon that as an excuse for further delaying Massasoit's messengers.
Squanto also knew that he ought to be turned over
to his own people and stoically consented to that
course, if the governor should so decide. To Massasoit and his messengers Bradford only argued his
usefulness, which was unquestionably great, and the
governor's evasiveness nearly cost the colony the
friendship of Massasoit. That Squanto was actuated by his own selfish and ambitious designs was
apparent to the authorities; for about this time in
consequence of the incident of the spring of 1622,
and Hobamock's report of "many secret passages
between Squanto and other Indians," as well as
other things that came to their attention, Bradford

says: "They began to see that Tisquantum sought his owne ends and plaid his owne game, by putting the Indians in fear, and drawing gifts from them to enrich himselfe; making them believe he could stir up war against whom he would and make peace for whom he would. Yea, he made them believe they kept the plague buried in the ground and could send it amongst whom they would, which did much terrifie the Indians, and made them depend more on him, and seeke more to him than to Massasoyte; which procured him envye, and had like to have cost him his life. For after the discovery of his practices, Massasoit sought it both privately and openly; which caused him to stick close to the English, and never durst goe from them till he dyed."

Fully appreciating the value of Squanto's assistance to the people of Plymouth, the searcher after truth cannot ignore the fact that his ambitious scheming probably came near to costing them their lives. The plot of the Massachusetts and other tribes in the spring of 1623 which was foiled by Standish and his indomitable eight, would undoubtedly not have been revealed but for Massasoit's restoration to health at the hands of Winslow, and, if not nipped in the bud, would have been quite likely to have been attended with success. Massasoit's failure to disclose it earlier was clearly due to a doubt on his part of the sincerity of the professed friendship of the English, and that doubt was aroused by the conduct of the governor in protecting Squanto after his perfidy to his Great Sachem became known, contrary to the terms of Carver's and Massasoit's treaty. Squanto died before the full effect of his conduct, or before the possible effect of it became known, and sleeps in the grave where white men laid him with Christian rites. There let him rest, and let us not too severely criticise him. He was but following the dictates of a trait of human character, that, while inordinately developed in the race of American Indians, is common to all. Shakespeare makes Cardinal Wolsey say to his devoted follower, "Cromwell, I charge thee, fling away ambition. By that sin fell the angels. How then can mortal man hope to win by it?" We do not agree with this thought, but rather, how can mortal man win without it? The only difficulty is to direct it in the right paths and keep it within proper bounds. Neither of these was Squanto able to do. In the words of Parkman, let us attribute his act to the working of "the ordinary instincts of humanity" which "should be classed with the other enigmas of the fathomless heart."

During the brief space of his life after the discovery of his schemes, the English took full advantage of this jealousy between him and Hobamock to secure better service from both by playing them against each other, — the governor "seeming to countenance one and Standish the other."

Like Squanto, we are told that Hobamock remained with the English until he died. The last mention made of him by Bradford is in connection with the Day of Humiliation in July, 1623. Like Squanto, too, he was of invaluable assistance to the

English, unquestionably of much greater service in their trading expeditions among the tribes on the cape and around Massachusetts Bay, by reason of his rank and standing in his own tribe, than he could otherwise have been, the mere fact that he was one of Massasoit's "chiefest men of valor" and war counsellors, adding to his prestige and the standing of the men for whom he virtually stood sponsor.

Thus passed from the stage three men whose activities had such a marked influence upon the earliest successful attempt at colonization in New England that their names and deeds are known to thousands of American children who probably could not name the first three governors of the Plymouth Colony.

VIII

THE NARRAGANSETTS

WHEN Winslow and Hopkins visited Sowams in July, 1621, they learned from the Pokanokets that across the bay lived a powerful federation that had not been touched by the plague. We find them sometimes referred to by early writers as Narrowhansetts, which perhaps was as nearly correct as the Englishman who heard the name spoken could reproduce the sound. The spelling was subsequently changed to Nariganset and finally to Narragansett, and it is by this latter name that they are known to history. We are told, on authority as reliable as any we have concerning the Indian tribes of New England, that they numbered twenty or twenty-five thousand with a war strength of from three to five thousand, and occupied all the territory westerly from Narragansett Bay and Providence River to the Pequot country, which extended to Wecapoag about five or six miles east of the Paucatuc River, the dividing line between Connecticut and Rhode Island.

The Narragansetts formed the second of the five great federations of New England Indians as enumerated by Gookin, and dignified by Drake with the designation Great Sachemries. They had undoubtedly been visited by the English before 1621; some writers, as we have already seen, claiming that the episode of Captain Waymouth with the Indians in 1605, as related by Rofier, occurred in the Narragansett country. The French frequented the bay for fishing according to the information given to Winslow by the people of Sowams, and so they were not unacquainted with the whites.

Hutchinson says Tashtussuch was their Chief Sachem when the English arrived. If this is true he did not long remain in that position after their arrival, his grandson Canonicus being at the head of the federation in the summer of 1621. It is related of Tashtussuch that he had two children, a son and a daughter, and, being unable to match them according to their station and dignity, he joined them in marriage. Four sons were born of this union of whom Canonicus was the oldest, and Mascus, the father of Miantonomo, the youngest. Miantonomo succeeded his uncle Canonicus, and, after his murder on Sachem's Plain, he was in turn succeeded by his brother Pessacus, who was said to have been only twenty years old when he assumed the chieftaincy. Pessacus was succeeded by Miantonomo's son Canonchet who was the leader of the federation in King Philip's war, and who met the same fate as his father. By what law of descent the chieftaincy passed from Miantonomo to his brother and then back to his own line again, we do not know; unless the line was simply preserved for Miantonomo's son by some sort of regency during his minority; or unless the Great Chieftaincy was an elective position, or a great Sachem had the power to name his successor, both of which suggestions will hereafter receive further consideration.

Pessacus is probably better known to history as Canonicus, his appearance under that name after the death of the first Canonicus, and especially after the death of Miantonomo, leading to some confusion of him with his grandfather by those who read only superficially. Another son of Mascus was Meika, who was also called by several other names, and was probably the Mishuano who married a daughter of Ninigret, named Magnus, later known as the "Sunke Squaw" or "Old Queen of the Narragansetts."

That Canonicus, who was at the head of the federation in 1621, was a great warrior seems to be generally conceded, although almost nothing has been handed down to indicate the way in which he earned the reputation, or the particular wars in which he engaged. The Pequots on the west must have caused him some trouble to prevent them from pushing further to the east than they did; and he did not live in peace and harmony with the Pokanokets across the bay at all times. Of his people it is asserted by some writers that they were related to the Mohicans, and by others that they were related to the Niantics, both of which statements are probably true in the sense that they were all Algonquins of the Wolf totem, as indeed were all the New England Indians. Their relationship to these two tribes may have been closer than with some of the others in point of time of their branch-

ing off from the parent stock; and one is sometimes
led to ask how much any one really knows about
the matter, as we find Ninigret spoken of by some
writers as a Niantic Sachem and by others as a
Narragansett, and the leader of the tribes of the
latter federation that joined the English in King
Philip's war. Whatever relationship there may
have been between them, if we are to accept as
final a very doubtful conclusion of early writers, it
was not close enough to allay the alleged jealousy of
Miantonomo, who had succeeded his uncle Canonicus as Chief Sachem of the Narragansetts, over the
division of the remnant of the Pequots among the
three tribes at the conclusion of the Pequot war;
nor to prevent the Mohicans under Uncas from
becoming the "most deadly enemies of the Narragansetts," when the former, by reason of the destruction of the Pequots, became the dominant tribe
in the old Pequot, later the Mohican, federation.

The settlers were to hear from them again very
shortly, for in November, 1621, Canonicus sent one
of his men, accompanied by a friendly Indian
named Tokamahamon, probably a Pokanoket,
to Plymouth, with a bundle of arrows tied in a
rattlesnake's skin. Squanto and Hobamock were
both absent at the time of their arrival, and the
Governor decided to detain the messenger until
their return. In the meantime "Captain Standish
tried to find out from him what it meant. He said
he did not surely know, but thought it meant hostilities." Standish and Hopkins finally succeeded
in allaying his fears, and induced him to talk;

whereupon he told them that the messenger whom Canonicus had sent in the summer to treat of peace, upon his return "persuaded him rather to war, and, to the end that he might provoke him thereunto, detained many of the presents sent to Canonicus, scorning the meanness of them, both in respect of what he had sent the English and the greatness of Canonicus."

He assured them that "upon the knowledge of the false carriage of the former messenger it would cost him his life," and that "upon the relation of their speech then with him, to his master, he would be friends with the Pilgrims." Squanto, having returned, then interpreted the message in the same way that the bearer of it had done. Governor Bradford took the skin, filled it with powder and shot and returned it to Canonicus, with a message of defiance, and invited him to a trial of strength. Canonicus refused to receive it and sent it back to Plymouth, and thus trouble was averted.

I have told the story as related by Bradford, but I find that some writers put it a little differently, fixing the time as February, 1622, and saying that Canonicus' messenger left the challenge and retired. At any rate, the governor's defiance had the desired effect and the English were not molested by the Narragansetts for fifteen years; although we are told by Bradford that the English were in great fear of them in 1622.

In his description of the building of a fort at Plymouth in the summer of that year, after describing the fort in detail, he says: "It served them also as a meeting house, and was fitted accordingly for that use. It was a great work for them in this weakness and time of wants; but the danger of the time required it, and both the continual rumors of the fears from the Indians here, especially the Narigansets, and also the hearing of that great massacre in Virginia made all hands willing to despatch the same."

In 1632, war broke out between the Narragansetts and the Wampanoags in which the former were, without doubt, the aggressors. The English, as in duty bound by their original treaty with Massasoit, came to the aid of their allies, the Wampanoags, and the war was of very short duration.

The first serious affair that threatened discord between the whites and the Narragansetts directly, was the murder of John Oldham in 1636. Oldham had sailed to Connecticut to trade with the Pequots, and on his return had been murdered by Indians at Munisses (Block Island). These Indians were Narragansetts, and one early writer suggests that they were probably angered by the fact that Oldham was engaged in trade with their most deadly enemies. Upon complaint of this atrocity being made by the whites to Canonicus, he sent his nephew, Miantonomo, with two hundred men to punish the offenders.

Canonicus and Miantonomo succeeded in satisfying the colonists that this was the act of some reckless members of the tribe, and that they were not concerned in it; and returned Oldham's two boys, who were taken prisoners at the time of his death, and had been held by their captors.

On October 21, 1636, Miantonomo with two sons of
Canonicus and twenty other Indians went to Boston to give notice of the threatening attitude of the
Pequots; and while there entered into an agreement
with the authorities by which each side bound itself
not to make peace with the Pequots without the
consent of the other.

Following close on the heels of this warning by
the friendly Narragansetts came confirmation of the
word brought to Boston by Miantonomo; for on
February 22, 1637, the Pequots attacked Saybrook
and on April 12, Weathersfield, both in Connecticut.
During this period Miantonomo had received other
information which he deemed of sufficient importance to send messengers to Boston to impart to the
authorities there; for at some time during the early
spring he sent word that, following a custom among
the Indians before an impending war of great mag-
nitude, the Pequots had sent their women and children away to an island. A force of forty men was
thereupon raised and sent to Narragansett to join
Miantonomo's warriors in an advance against the
Pequots. Aside from the part played by the Narragansetts in the attack upon the Pequot fortress,
any account of this war would be out of place in
this chapter.

Historians tell us that the Narragansetts were of
very little service in the attack upon the Pequot
fort, holding themselves aloof and contenting themselves with stopping such as fled. It is inconceivable that Narragansett warriors, who have never been
accused of cowardice in the face of their enemies,

led by such men as were at their head at that time, would refuse or hesitate to go against their mortal foes, when aided by the English, without some good cause; and this well-known propensity of theirs to mingle in the thickest of the fighting lends color to their claim that they had been slighted by the English; and that Miantonomo, after performing good service, had been insulted and even threatened with bodily injury. It must be borne in mind in this connection that the Mohicans under Uncas fought with the Connecticut troops in this war; and that the natives were inordinately jealous of any slight placed upon their cheifs or tribe. It is among the possibilities that the Mohicans, and Uncas, their sachem, being on very friendly terms with Captain Mason, the commander of the expedition, may have received some recognition or consideration at the hands of the whites that was not extended to the Narragansetts and their chief. Probably nothing would sooner kindle their resentment, as they were the much more powerful federation of the two; their chief came of an illustrious ancestry; and they, like most other Indians, were likely to consider themselves a little superior to their neighbors. If this surmise is correct, it was the fault of the whites themselves that they received no assistance from the Narragansetts; for they had lived among the Indians long enough to have learned this trait of their character, and they should have avoided anything that would arouse the jealousy of one of their allies as against the other. With them a slight would be an insult to their chief, and

the threat of bodily injury might have followed
some protest on his part against the treatment of
his people, and resulted from it. If the Indian
claim of insult is well founded, it shows a woful lack
of diplomacy on the part of the whites, and their
usual utter failure to manifest any appreciation of
favors done or services rendered; for it was Miantonomo himself who had gone to Boston in October
to warn the English, and had sent word of the removal of the Pequot women and children, and apprised the authorities of what such a removal meant.

Besides, Bradford tells us that in 1636 there had
been a war between the Pequots and the Narragansetts, saying, "these Narigansets held correspond-
ance and termes of friendship with the English of
the Massachusetts." In this war the Mohicans undoubtedly fought with the Pequots, being of their
federation, and the Narragansetts probably saw in
their abandonment of the then titular head of the
federation a crafty scheme on the part of Uncas to
overthrow Sassacus, as he had several times before
attempted to do, and place his own tribe in the
dominant position, and himself at the head of the
nation, supported by English muskets in the hands
of English soldiers. That this was a fact was subsequently clearly demonstrated.

Bradford also tells us that following the truce
after this war Governor Vane of Plymouth, with
Roger Williams' assistance, made a treaty with the
Narragansetts. This would be at about the same
time that Miantonomo made the treaty with the
authorities of the Massachusetts Bay Colony, of

which I have already written. These are the first
formal treaties between the whites and the Narragansetts of which I find any record, unless we are
to dignify the agreement before referred to with
the name of a treaty.

At the conclusion of the Pequot war in which
they were practically wiped out, some two hundred
survivors were distributed among the Mohicans,
Niantics and Narragansetts. This division is said
to have angered the Narragansetts, and is given as
a reason for an alleged attempt on the part of the
latter to raise a general conspiracy against the
English in 1640, the details of which belong more
properly in the chapter devoted to Miantonomo.

1643 was the year of Miantonomo's ill-fated
expedition against the Mohicans. Sequassen, a Sachem of the Connecticut Valley, apparently not connected with any of the great federations, unless
DeForest's conclusion that all the tribes of Western Connecticut were related to the Narragansetts is correct, was friendly to Miantonomo and
hostile to Uncas. Some difficulty arising between
him and Uncas over the killing of one of the subjects
of the latter by one of Sequassen's men, and an
alleged attempt upon the life of Uncas by shooting
at him while he was paddling his canoe in the Connecticut River, Uncas, as usual, instead of taking
the matter into his own hands, neither he nor Sequassen being under the guardianship of the English,
complained to the authorities at Hartford, claiming
that, for this and other acts, he ought to have six
of Sequassen's men that he might put them to

death. The authorities for some unaccountable reason thought this unfair, and the governor finally induced him to be content with the man who had committed the murder. I say for some unaccountable reason, because a careful reading of the history of that time leads one to the conclusion that the Connecticut authorities, frequently aided by those of the Massachusetts colonies, seemed more intent upon aiding the Mohicans than upon doing justice; and I am at a loss to understand this lapse from their usual policy.

But, to return to the assassin, he was found to be a friend and relative of Miantonomo, and Sequassen refused to give him up, probably relying on the Narragansetts to support him. And again the magistrates showed remarkable acumen, for, being unable to effect a reconciliation, they dismissed both Uncas and Sequassen, advising Uncas, however, to avenge his own grievances. Uncas thereupon invaded Sequassen's territory, burned and plundered as he went, and killed some seven or eight men and wounded others.

Miantonomo was not the kind of man to sit by and see his allies treated in this manner without taking some action looking towards their assistance, and he accordingly complained to Uncas' friends, the authorities of Connecticut. The governor refused to interfere; and Miantonomo gave notice to the governor of Massachusetts Bay, and inquired if the people of Massachusetts would be offended if he made war against the Mohicans. This notice and inquiry was in strict compliance with the terms of the treaty he had made with them. The governor replied, "If Uncas had done him or his friends any wrong, and had refused to grant satisfaction, the English would leave him to choose his own course."

He then collected a force of nine hundred or a thousand warriors and marched to the Connecticut Valley. Uncas went out to meet him and adopted just such a course as one would expect of him. He asked for a conference with Miantonomo between the two opposing forces (a virtual truce) and Miantonomo, with the honor of his race, believing that his enemy would adhere to its traditions and customs, granted his request. Uncas then submitted a proposition that he knew Miantonomo would not accept, and which he probably would not have made if he had believed it would be accepted. He proposed that the two chiefs settle the conflict by a personal combat between them. Miantonomo refused, saying, "my men came to fight and they shall fight." Uncas then fell to the ground, this being the prearranged signal for a shower of arrows from three hundred Mohican bows against their unprepared enemies who were within easy shot, and entirely unsuspicious of any such an act of perfidy.

This is the incident of which Bradford writes that Miantonomo "came suddenly upon him with nine or ten hundred men, never denouncing any war before. Uncas had only about half so many but it pleased God to give Uncas the victory." If they believed that the God they worshipped was "pleased" with such treachery as this, it may explain their own treatment of the Indians; and as to

the Narragansetts "never denouncing any war before," I am unable to find any record of Uncas'
"denouncing any war" before he invaded the territory of Sequassen, Miantonomo's weak ally, and
killing his men and laying waste his country; or,
for that matter, of the Plymouth authorities themselves "denouncing any war" at a later date when
they sent Major Winslow with an armed force to
seize Wamsutta in his own domain and bring him
to Plymouth at the point of a loaded pistol, because
of some suspicion.

When the shower of arrows fell upon them the
Narragansetts fled. Miantonomo was wearing an
English corselet which impeded his flight, and some
pursuing Mohicans contented themselves with getting in his way so as to hinder him further, in order
that Uncas himself, who appears not to have been
in the front ranks of the pursuers, might have the
honor of taking him. The story of Miantonomo's
fate belongs in another place; and I will pass on to
the effect of his murder upon the Narragansetts.

The following winter the Indians on the Connecticut River, probably Sequassen's men, made much
trouble; and the Narragansetts urged the Governor
of Massachusetts "that they be allowed to make
war upon Uncas, saying he had received a ransom for
Miantonomo's life and then executed him; but permission was refused, and they were put off with a
promise that if it was shown that ransom had been
received they would cause Uncas to return the
same."

With their usual happy faculty for believing

what they wanted to, the colonial council decided the issue against the Narragansetts. The latter, unable to get any satisfaction, then signed an agreement not to open hostilities until the next planting of corn, and even then to give the English thirty days notice. Bradford says they also agreed that "if any of the Nayantick Pequots should make any assault upon Uncas or any of his, they would give them up to the English to be punished, and that they would not procure the Mowacks to come against him during this truce."

I have spoken of this agreement as of the time of the Narragansetts' complaint in the winter following Miantonomo's death, although some writers fix the time of its making as coincident with the mockery of a trial that was accorded to Miantonomo.

These events occurred in the summer of 1643 and the winter following; and, in 1645, the trouble between the two federations broke out again with fresh violence, of which Roger Williams wrote to Winslow on June 25th of that year as follows: "The Narragansets and Monhiggens, with their respective confederates, have deeply implunged themselves in barbarous slaughter. For myself, I have (to my utmost) diswaded our neighbours high and low from armes, etc. but there is a spirit of desperacion fallen upon them, resolved to revenge the death of their prince, and recover the ransom for his life, etc. or to perish with him."

Following this outbreak the Colonists patched up some sort of a truce between the Narragansetts and Niantics on the one hand and the Mohicans on the other, as usual placing all the burden on the former; for they succeeded in some way, not made entirely clear, in getting the signatures of their leaders to an agreement to keep the peace with the English United Colonies, Uncas and others, without requiring the Mohicans to keep their hands off the Narragansetts or their allies west of the Connecticut River. This was signed by Pessacus, who, as we have seen, was a brother of Miantonomo and succeeded him as Chief Sachem of the federation, Meekesano, probably Meika or Mishuanno, another brother of Miantonomo, who had married Magnus the "Old Queen of the Narragansetts" who participated in King Philip's war, and Witowash, all described as Sachems of the Narragansetts, Annesquem, deputy of the Niantics, Abdas, Pummash and Cutchamakin.

The spirit of the Narragansetts seems to have been broken by their failure to secure any satisfaction or justice from the English, and for the thirty-two years ensuing, before King Philip's war, they confined their hostilities to constant attacks upon the Mohicans and to acts of depredation against the whites and especially the clergy, upon whom they wreaked a terrible vengeance for their participation in the farcical trial and subsequent death of their beloved Miantonomo.

When King Philip, roused to frenzy by the injustice of the English, rose in arms in 1675, all the Narragansetts except a few tribes under the old Sachem Ninigret, who joined with the English in the destruction of his countrymen, sided with Philip and played the part of men, meeting their fate like the brave warriors they were. I say except Ninigret, for while he is spoken of as a Narragansett Sachem, there is little, or perhaps no doubt in my mind that he was not a true Narragansett, but a Niantic driven with his people across the Paucatuc by the Pequots, and living there on Narragansett territory under the protection of the Sachems of that federation.

I have spoken of the advancement made by the Narragansetts in common with the Wampanoags, and it is of interest to note in this connection that DeForest, who is exceedingly skeptical concerning the figures given by early historians in speaking of the numerical strength of the various federations, says that their territory was probably more densely populated than any other part of the United States, and, while he attributes this fact to the excellent fishing about Narragansett Bay, which enabled more of them to live there than in other places, it should be borne in mind that this bay had no monopoly on fishing, Samoset leading the Plymouth settlers to the shores of Maine for fish, and Cape Cod Bay itself being a fishing resort of the English before the settlement at Plymouth. The true reason for the density of the population, which before the plague undoubtedly extended to the Pokanoket and Pocasset territory of the Wampanoags, probably lies in the fact that these federations were more advanced in agriculture than the other Algonquin tribes. In fact, DeForest says, the Narragansett men, unlike most of the race, did not shirk manual labor. He also speaks of them as of a much milder and more humane disposition than the Pequots and Mohicans.

Under the guiding hand of the few English who appear to have been interested in them as men, and not simply as cumberers of the earth which the English coveted, they made rapid progress toward civilization. It was the Narragansetts that gave refuge to the persecuted Quakers from Massachusetts Bay. It was to them that Roger Williams fled when he was banished from Salem in 1636, after spending a part of the winter at Sowams; and it was among them that Williams lived, loved and respected by them for more than forty years. It was to them that Gorton fled with his dissenting or heterodox associates when banished from Plymouth; and Deane thinks the council of clergymen who decided Miantonomo's fate may have been influenced by the fact that the Narragansetts gave him refuge. There is reason for his conclusion in the fact, already referred to, that these men who had fled from the old world to the wilderness of the new to be free from the restrictions placed upon their religious belief and religious thought, as soon as they had found the haven they sought, became as intolerant of dissenters from their views as the clergy of the established church had ever been of them. In a word they were especially zealous to deprive others of the same liberty they came here to secure for themselves.

The part played by the Narragansetts under the leadership of Pumham, Canonchet, Quinapen and the "Old Queen," in King Philip's war, the defection of Ninigret, and his aid to the English in that war, which resulted in the extermination of his people, belongs more properly in another place, and I will pass to the consideration of the greatest chieftain produced by the federation during the short period of its existence of which anything is known.

IX

MIANTONOMO

THIS Great Sachem of the Narragansetts, as we have seen, was a nephew of Canonicus, whose activities in the early days of the colonies have been briefly adverted to, and the great grandson of Tashtussuch. Notwithstanding the fact that Canonicus had two sons at least, who are mentioned in history as having accompanied Miantonomo to Boston in 1636, and who fought with him at Sachem's Plain, where they were both wounded, Miantonomo, the son of Canonicus' youngest brother Mascus, was his war captain and trusted counsellor before he laid down the tomahawk, and his successor in the Great Chieftaincy. It was Miantonomo whom he sent to punish the murderers of Oldham in 1636, and it was Miantonomo who headed the party that traveled to Boston on October 21 of the same year to apprise the English of the threatening attitude of the Pequots.

While we are not familiar with the laws of descent among the Algonquins, gathering our information from all available sources, and drawing such inferences as seem warranted by known facts, it would seem that the Narragansetts had a different rule than the other federations. We see Passaconaway of the Pawtuckets succeeded by his son Wonolan-

cet; Sassacus of the Pequots following his father
Wopigwooit, and Oweneco of the Mohicans taking
up the reins his father Uncas laid down. We find
Massasoit of the Wampanoags succeeded in the
Great Chieftaincy of that federation by his eldest
son Wamsutta, and the latter followed by his
younger brother Pometacom, while Canonicus is
succeeded by a son of his youngest brother, passing
over his own sons and possibly those of two other
brothers. If there was any uniform rule it must
have been that the Great Sachem named his own
successor from the warriors of his blood and family,
or that the royal family selected their Great Sachem
from their own number.*

If either method was pursued, Miantonomo must
have been a man of parts, either to have been
named by his uncle in preference to his own sons,
or to have secured the election from among the
many men who were eligible to the position. We
have seen much of his friendliness towards the
whites; and there is yet much to be said concerning
him and his activities during the short space of
not more than seven years of his great chieftaincy.

In 1636, after a truce had been declared between
the Pequots and the Narragansetts, Roger Williams
reported to Governor Winthrop of Massachusetts
Bay that Miantonomo had told him that the Pequots had labored with the Narragansetts to persuade them that the English were minded to destroy
all Indians. This may have been only a trick of the
wily Sassacus to arouse the other federation to join

* See note at end of chapter.

him in the uprising he was then planning; but the
events of the next forty years showed that Sassacus,
if he was sincere in his belief, had read the English
character and foresaw the result of their continued
occupancy of more and more of the Indian lands,
better than any of the other Sachems of his time.
This incident is related here simply for the purpose
of calling attention to the sincerity of Miantonomo's
friendship or his apparent sagacity in forewarning
the whites against his own most deadly foes in the
hope of compassing their destruction. The chances
are strongly in favor of the first of these alterna-
tives, because the total annihilation of the Pequots
would only result in bringing some other tribe of
the federation to the front, still having a powerful,
though somewhat reduced, nation on his western
border which was likely to be just as hostile.

In 1638, Arthur Peach and three accomplices
killed a Narragansett Indian who had been to Massachusetts Bay to trade, and they were taken at
Aquidnick by order of Roger Williams. Williams
learned from friendly Indians of the same tribe that
"the natives, friends of the slain man, had consulta-
tion to kill an Englishman in revenge." Miantonomo also heard of this, whether through Williams
or from his own people does not appear, and he
sent word to the English, urging them to be careful
when on the highways, and at the same time
threatened his own people with punishment if they
took the matter of vengeance into their own hands,
telling them the governor (of Plymouth) would
see justice done, as indeed he did in this case,

hanging Peach and two of his accomplices, the other escaping to Piscataqua where the settlers protected him.

In 1640 rumors reached Boston that Miantonomo was breeding dissension, and was trying to incite the tribes to a general rebellion against the whites. "Rebellion" is the word used by the early writers; but my understanding of the term is that it means a revolt against lawful authority, and by what process of reasoning the colonial governments of that day concluded that they had any lawful authority over the Indians is beyond my comprehension. Why the Massachusetts authorities failed to take account of the past, of Miantonomo's sincerity, which had been so often manifested, and of Uncas' well-known duplicity, in the controversy between them, which was almost constantly before the English magistrates from that time until Miantonomo's death, is another of the mysteries for which history offers no solution; and their constant support of Uncas, and abandonment of the man whose character was so much above that of Uncas that there is no comparison between them, places a blot upon the pages of the history of that period that time cannot efface, an indelible stain upon their judicial ermine.

When these rumors reached Boston in 1640, Miantonomo was summoned to appear before the governor of Massachusetts Bay, the English or colonial authorities pursuing their usual high-handed methods of ordering men who were not under their jurisdiction around as though they were subject

to them. Whatever may have been Miantonomo's feelings about their assumption of authority
over him, he suppressed them, and went to
Boston, undoubtedly willing to go the whole distance, and not merely half way, in an effort to preserve the peace and show his readiness to observe
the terms of his treaties and agreements with the
whites. When he presented himself before the
governor he demanded an investigation, and that
his accusers be called to confront him, and if found
to be in the wrong that they be put to death. He
averred that Uncas and the Mohicans had become
his enemies and were circulating this slander against
him. Nothing was shown implicating him in any
wrongdoing, but the circulation of the rumors resulted in a most bitter enmity between him and
Uncas, which was terminated only by Miantonomo's
fall at the hands of the most treacherous Redskin
that the New England tribes produced during the
period covered by our knowledge of them, aided
and abetted by the men Miantonomo had befriended.

This enmity probably extended to the Connecticut tribes that were more friendly to Miantonomo
than to Uncas, including the Niantics and such of
the old Pequot tribe as had been absorbed by them;
and was unquestionably responsible for an alleged
attempt upon the life of Uncas who claimed to
have been shot at and wounded in the arm by an
arrow from the bow of some unknown person, if
any such attempt was actually made. At about
this time a young Pequot was found to be in possession of more wampum than it was thought he ought

to have, and he fled to the Narragansetts who protected him. Uncas rushed to the colonial authorities again, as usual, with this fresh complaint, and Miantonomo was once more called to Boston. On a hearing upon Uncas' complaint, Miantonomo called the Pequot as a witness, and he told in detail of a plot on the part of Uncas to involve Miantonomo. He said that Uncas had tried to induce him to tell the English that Miantonomo had employed him to kill Uncas; and that the latter, to give color to the charge, took a flint from his gun and cut his arm on both sides to make it appear as if an arrow had gone through it. The English, as usual, refused to believe this, and ordered Miantonomo to give the Pequot up to Uncas, another case of their assumption of authority they did not possess; "intending to subject him to their vengeance." Miantonomo, still desirous of avoiding trouble, acquiesced, but claimed the right of returning the Pequot to his own hunting grounds as he had introduced him. This was allowed, and some of Miantonomo's men started out with him to return him, but themselves killed him while on the way, an act of mercy on their part which ought to commend itself to any one with a spark of humanity, for the Narragansetts knew what Mohican vengeance meant.

I use the expression "as usual" in speaking of the Massachusetts authorities' refusal to credit the testimony of the witness introduced on behalf of Miantonomo because this seems to have been their constant policy. Miantonomo had repeatedly shown his friendship and good will towards them, they

never had a particle of evidence of any breach of
faith on his part, except such as was furnished by
his most inveterate foe, the most resourceful liar of
the times, but they persistently refused to listen to
evidence in his behalf, prefering to accept the
stories circulated by his enemy whom they knew to
be constantly plotting his overthrow, and whom
they knew equally well to be untrustworthy. The
only plausible explanation I can find for their attitude towards these two chiefs, who were no more to
be compared than are noonday and midnight, is
that Uncas was a ready tool in their hands for the
carrying out of their schemes against the other
Indians, in the police parlance of the day a stool
pigeon; or that the Narragansetts were more to
be feared than the Mohicans in case of an open
rupture.

And Uncas' reason for playing this part was to
secure the overthrow of the other Great Sachems
of the vicinity, to reduce their federations to a state
of vassalage, with himself the great Indian King of
the day, supported by English soldiers. He had
neither the prowess in battle, the mental qualities
or the personality to accomplish this without such
assistance; and there was no reason for all the
alleged attempts upon his life. The hostility was
not entirely personal, although Miantonomo had
good reason for a strong personal enmity to him;
but there was more than individual hostility involved. It was the hostility of one nation against
another, and if any of the numerous alleged attempts upon the life of Uncas had been successful,

it would only have resulted in putting in his place
another man who probably would have pursued his
policy. Again, there were so many complaints by
Uncas of these plots against his person, rather than
against his federation, that it seems remarkable
that the English did not become suspicious concerning them; but if they had any such suspicion they
carefully concealed it, and always found the issue,
when one was presented, in favor of Uncas. If all
the attempts to remove him, complained of, and
enumerated by Bradford, were actually made, there
must have been some exceedingly poor shots and
weak hands among the conspirators against him;
or he must have been even more skilled in magic,
or under the special protection of the Great Spirit
than was the celebrated Passaconaway.

After the capture of Miantonomo, as already related, Uncas endeavored to extort from him a plea
for his life, saying that if he were Miantonomo's
prisoner he would beg for mercy at his hands, all
of which was undoubtedly true. Failing by this
means to force a word from the lips of the Great
Chief, who throughout displayed the stoicism of his
race, Uncas then caused some of the Narragansett
warriors, who had been taken prisoners, to be
brought up and tomahawked before his eyes. Even
this, evidently intended as an object lesson of what
was in store for him, failed to move him to the
utterance of a word. Uncas then, well knowing
that a trial before English judges was equivalent to
conviction and execution for Miantonomo, and to
shirk the responsibility for his death, referred the

case to the English who had just effected a union under the name of the "United Colonies of New England," and had provided for the appointment of two commissioners each from Massachusetts Bay, Plymouth, Connecticut and New Haven, to consider matters of common interest. The first Commissioners named for the several colonies were as follows: Massachusetts Bay, John Winthrop and Thomas Dudley; Plymouth, Edward Winslow and William Collier; Connecticut, George Fenwick and Edward Hopkins; New Haven, Theophilus Eaton and Thomas Gregson.

Bradford relates that at their first meeting held September 7, 1643, at Boston, "amongst other things they had this matter of great consequence to consider on; the Narigansets, after the subduing of the Pequentes thought to have ruled over all the Indians about them; but the English especially those of Conightecutt, holding correspondence and friendship with Uncass, Sachem of the Monhigg Indeans which lived nere them (as the Massachusetts had done with the Narigansets) and he had been faithful to them in the Pequente Warr, they were ingaged to support him in his just liberties, and were contented that such of the surviving Pequentes as had submitted to him should remain with him and under his protection. This increased his power to such an extent that it was unendurable to the Narigansets and Miantonomo, their Chief Sachem (an ambitious and politick man) and he sought privately and by treachery (according to the Indian manner) to make way with him by hiring some to kill him. Some sought to poyson him, to knock him in the head in his own house and to shoot him and such like attempts. None of these taking effect, he made open warr (contrary to the covenants between the English and the Narigansetts and the Mohicans and Narigansets)."

Bradford, and other writers following his conclusions, seems not to take account of the fact that the Mohicans, even if augmented by all the surviving Pequots, would have been no match for the Narragansetts. It requires but the application of a little common sense to known facts to refute all this nonsense about Miantonomo's jealousy on this score, and about the increase of Uncas' power by this means to such an extent "as to be unendurable" to the Narragansetts. The two hundred survivors of the Pequot warriors had been distributed, one hundred to the Mohicans, eighty to the Narragansetts, and twenty to the Niantics; and the Niantics were more friendly towards Miantonomo than to Uncas at that time. Then why all the talk about Miantonomo's jealousy and the increase of Uncas' power? He also apparently forgets, or did not know, that in "making open warr," Miantonomo took the counsel of the Massachusetts Bay authorities, and so it was not "contrary to the covenants between the English and the Narragansets."

Bradford simply follows the report of the Commissioners, and later writers follow Bradford; and it is not difficult to guess that the Commissioners were hard put to it for an excuse for deciding in Uncas' favor; and found it in this alleged jealousy of the increase of Uncas' power; that is, jealousy of something that did not exist unless Uncas was harboring other Pequots than those assigned to him. The Commissioners' report was so worded as to justify the dastardly act recommended by their five scape-goats and perpetrated by themselves. Upon what evidence they found the facts they do not say, nor is it necessary. A careful reading of history will convince any fair-minded man that Uncas had devoted six years to scheming and planning the overthrow of the enemy he dared not face in fair fight, preferring to rely upon the favor of the English; and that every complaint he ever made against Miantonomo was deliberately framed for that purpose.

It was on the evidence of Uncas' witnesses that the alleged facts were established. The Commissioners, unwilling to assume the responsibility for deciding a matter upon which they had probably already agreed, called in fifty clergymen, who were holding a conference at the time, and who chose five of their number to decide the fate of the Narragansett Sachem. Thus the question of life or death was left to five men who were willing to be made the scape-goats, and who belonged to the profession that subsequently showed itself to be made up of the most blood-thirsty of all the English, and even more so than any of those whom they delighted in calling savages.

Who the five men were history does not relate, probably because they feared the vengeance of the outraged Narragansetts; but they decided in favor of Uncas, and the Commissioners then passed sentence; that is, they authorized Uncas to put Miantonomo to death, advising moderation in the manner of his execution; and promised to assist Uncas if the Narragansetts or others should unjustly assault them for the execution. As if any assault upon them or upon their accomplices, the whites, for the execution, could be unjust. One is naturally led to ask why the English meddled in the affair at all. The only plausible answer is that they sought to terrify the natives for their own advantage.

Bradford informs us that "Uncass followed this advice, and accordingly executed him in a very faire manner, according as they advised, with due respect to his honor and greatness." And he might have added that Uncas paid a high tribute to his murdered foe in cutting a slice of flesh from his still quivering body and eating it, declaring, "it is the sweetest meat I ever ate. It makes my heart strong."

One piece of the evidence upon which the issue was decided is of sufficient importance to warrant a word of comment. When the people of Rhode Island, who lived near Miantonomo, and whom he had often befriended, took sides with him, believing him to be mainly in the right, Uncas' followers told the authorities at Hartford that Miantonomo had engaged the Mohawks to join him and that they were then encamped within a day's journey of the frontier, and were awaiting Miantonomo's liberation. The authorities apparently swallowed this statement, without making any attempt to verify it, and used it as the deciding piece of so-called evidence; thus establishing the truth of the last part of the complaint made by King Philip to Governor Easton thirty-two years later, that if "twenty of their honest Indians testified that an Englishman had done them wrong it was as nothing, but if one of their worst Indians testified against any Indian or their King, when it pleased the English it was sufficient."

The decision of the Commissioners was kept secret until they were out of the reach of the tribes, otherwise the commission would probably have had an unhappy ending. As soon as they had had time to reach places of safety the authorities of Hartford took Miantonomo from the jail there, where he had been confined, and delivered him to Uncas and his brother Wawequa, and they started back with him to their own hunting grounds, one of the stipulations being that he was not to be executed within the jurisdiction of the colonists.

When they arrived at Sachem's Plain, where the Mohicans had met the Narragansetts and defeated them by the trick referred to in the preceding chapter, Wawequa stepped behind Miantonomo and at a signal from Uncas struck him down with a tomahawk. Then followed the incident of the eating of a slice of his flesh. They buried him there; a friend piled a heap of stones on the grave and it is said that for a hundred years every Narragansett who passed that way turned in sadness and added a stone to the heap upon his grave, until a large mound marked the place.

Compare this case with that presented a little later by the Narragansetts, who complained that Uncas had received a ransom for Miantonomo's life and then executed him, and asked, not to have Uncas brought in and executed if found guilty, but simply that the English would allow them to avenge their own wrongs. This request was refused, the Narragansetts being put off with a promise that if it was shown that Uncas had received a ransom they would cause him to return it; and then conveniently deciding the issue in his favor. Thirty pieces of silver against a life! A few spans of wampum against the man whose lands they coveted!

Winthrop's narrative of the farce that they called a trial conveys such a different impression of the merits of the controversy between Uncas and Miantonomo than does that of the Commissioners, that it gives rise to the suggestion already made that the latter reported the matter in such a way as to vindicate their participation in what all reliable authorities agree in pronouncing a cold-blooded murder.

And so perished Miantonomo, the best friend the whites had among the Indians after Massasoit; that is, if they valued the friendship of a man rather than that of a Mohican. Historians, except Bradford, agree that he was guiltless of any offence; he had many times shown the greatness of his character in his dealings with the whites; and when it came to a question of simple justice at their hands, it was refused, and he was given up to his most cruel enemy for assassination by a man who could not look him in the face when he struck the deadly blow.

After the condemnation of Miantonomo by a body of clergymen, is it any wonder that for the next hundred years more clergymen fell by the tomahawk in New England, in proportion to their numbers, than those of any other class? Is it any wonder that, instead of the peace the colonists pretended to expect to follow this unjustifiable act, they found themselves confronted by thirty years of reprisal and vengeance, terminating only in the extinction of the Narragansetts in King Philip's war?

If we are inclined to think the penalty exacted by the Indians severe, let us not lose sight of the fact that the offence was serious, and that the simple natives, unable to secure the colonists' consent to their exacting justice, took the matter into their own hands, and avenged their leader's death upon the heads of the accomplices to his murder.

Does any one wonder after reading the story of the Mohicans and Narragansetts, culminating in the death of the Narragansett Sachem, that the chiefs "had a great fear that any of their Indians should be called or forced to be Christians," as stated by Governor Easton?

I fancy there was a shade of irony in the wily old Ninigret's reply to Mayhew when he asked permission to preach among the old Sachem's people. "Make the English good first; try it on the Pequots and Mohicans and if it works, I will consider it."

Do we wonder that the Christian religion failed to impress Massasoit, who saw the practices of the Christian English, and who manifested more of the spirit of true Christianity than all the clergy of New England of his time, excepting John Eliot and Roger Williams?

Speaking of Miantonomo and his son Canonchet, Schoolcraft, who is not noted for many expressions of sympathy with the Indians or their cause, says: "His unjustifiable death on Sachem's Plain is not so remarkable as an act of savage cruelty as it is of English casuistry. An Indian was made to strike the executionary blow which Indian clemency or diplomacy had withheld. Canonchet also fell by the same questionable system."

Note. — Since writing this chapter I have received a suggestion that the sons of a great chief might lose their rights of succession by marrying beneath their station, a thought that had entirely escaped the writer's attention, but which seems entirely plausible.

X

THE PEQUOTS, MOHICANS AND OTHER WESTERN TRIBES

THE attention of the reader has already been called to the fact that Schoolcraft speaks of the "Wolf totem or Mohicans" as the first of the three clans of the Leni Lenapee or parent stock of the Algonquins to migrate from their ancestral hunting grounds, and that Gallatin thinks it was the only one to penetrate into strange lands. Whether either of these conjectures is right or wrong we do not certainly know, but Schoolcraft speaks with such positiveness of the identity of the "Wolfs" with the "Mahangins," as they seem to have been originally called, that it is probably safe to conclude that the Mohicans were of that totem and adopted as their national cognomen the name of the entire clan. If Gallatin is correct, we are, of course, led to the inevitable conclusion that all the tribes occupying the vast expanse of territory outlined in a preceding chapter, except those who continued to live around New Jersey, Delaware, Maryland and Eastern Pennsylvania, were originally Mahangins, who swept out to the north, the south, the east and the west in successive tides, and as they became separated from each other formed separate federa-

194

tions, all closely related, but having a sufficiently distinct existence, so that in the development of their customs and their language they eventually differed so materially that it has required extensive research by linguists into the common roots of their various dialects, of which there are said to have been more than forty, to classify them properly.

Whatever may have been the early scope of the name "Mahangin," at the beginning of the seventeenth century, Mohican was the name applied to a tribe of the Pequot nation as it was then called. If Schoolcraft's belief that the Pequots were true Mohicans is well founded, it would be more appropriate to speak of them as the Mohican Nation or federation, in which the Pequots, one of the tribes of the nation, had gained the ascendency. Other writers, however, assert that the Pequots were an inland tribe that had swept down and overwhelmed the Mohicans, whom they ruled as a conquered people. If this is true, they simply constituted another of those waves of migration to which I have referred, that rolled across the Nipmuck territory to the north and could not be stayed until they reached the shores of Long Island Sound, compelling the Mohicans who had occupied this territory to confine themselves to the northerly portion of their former hunting grounds, while they themselves settled down on the more desirable portions bordering on the water. These two theories are not irreconcilable, for, as we have seen, Gallatin says they were all "Mahangins."

Whatever may have been their origin or their

relationship, we find some writers who cover the earliest periods of American history speaking of the Pequot Nation as having their principal rallying place near the mouth of the Thames River, which was in the territory then occupied by the true Pequots, "where Connecticote, Quinnipoig and Sassacus" were called "the three Kings, of whom Sassacus was the most noted warrior, though Connecticote was the Chief of Chiefs." This is hardly reconcilable with other equally positive statements by other historians who tell us that Wopigwooit, sometimes called Pekoath, was the great chief of the federation until his death at the hands of Dutch traders about 1633. He was undoubtedly succeeded by his son Sassacus.

The question that naturally arises, then, is, who were the other of the three kings? And if Wopigwooit was the great chief as was his father before him, and he was succeeded by his son in the Great Chieftaincy, how does it come about that Connecticote was Chief of Chiefs? From what we know of the activities of the tribe from 1635 until its practical extermination in 1637, it seems safe to conclude that the other two kings mentioned were only the sachems of some subdivisions of the federation, perhaps of the royal line of Wopigwooit, and high counsellors of the War Lord Sassacus; although Quinnipoig is the name given by some writers to one of the Connecticut River tribes.

While Gookin and, following him, Drake, Gallatin and Schoolcraft give the name Pequot to the first of the five great nations of New England In-

dians, it is significant that the true Pequot territory
extended only from the Paucatuc River on the
east to the Niantic on the west, and from Long
Island Sound northerly less than half way across
the state of Connecticut. That their territory did
not extend westerly to the Connecticut River is
clearly established, for while they undoubtedly held
sway over the western Niantics, occupying the peninsula formed by the Niantic and Connecticut
Rivers, north of these lay the Podunks, whose Sachem Waghinacut went to Boston in 1631 to try to
induce the English to settle in the Connecticut
Valley. He boasted of the fertility of the soil and
offered to provide settlers with corn and to give
them eighty beaver skins if they would send a colony
into his territory. Winthrop says he afterwards
found that he was a very treacherous man and had
been at war with a far greater Sachem named Pekoath. DeForest, however, says the Pequots defeated them in their battles and compelled them to
submit to Pekoath.

The Podunks, as I have said, lay north of the
western Niantics on the east side of the Connecticut River. To be more accurate I should have said
they were north of the Wauguncks who occupied
the territory immediately north of the western
Niantics and also on the west side of the river.

I am aware that in placing the limit I do on the
Pequot territory, I am running against the claims
of some old writers who assert that Sassacus' sway
extended nearly to the Hudson River, as well as
the statement of others that he had twenty-six sub-

sachems or sagamores under him, because there were not twenty-six tribes in all Connecticut if the authorities that seem most reliable are to be believed; and Gallatin, who appears to have made extensive research to gather the material for his Archæologia Americana, says there were seven independent tribes west of the Connecticut River. DeForest, who published a history of the Connecticut Indians in 1852 under the auspices of the Connecticut Historical Society, shows a map of Connecticut as it was in 1630, on which he locates ten such tribes, naming them. If it should be claimed that these were really of the Pequot nation, we come right back to the fact that one of them had recently been at war with Pekoath (Wopigwooit) of the Pequots; and we are confronted with the further fact that the Tunxis, another of these tribes, if it was subject to Sassacus, did not constitute any part of the Mohican nation which Uncas built up on the ruins of the Pequot; for as we have already seen, Sequassen, their sachem, was more friendly to Miantonomo than to Uncas, and is said by DeForest to have been related to the Narragansett sachems.

This same Sequassen owned the land where Hartford now stands and sold it to the English. DeForest says these western Connecticut tribes were all numerically weak, but for that matter he places the strength of all the New England tribes at a much lower figure than other writers, estimating the Pequots at three hundred warriors, the number seen by Endicott when he was on the coast in 1636, rather than seven hundred as given by Captain

Mason who overthrew them in 1637, and whose figures are generally accepted; and the Narragansetts he gives but ten to twelve hundred warriors against the three to four thousand as credited to them by other writers, except Gookin who places them at one thousand.

DeForest further contradicts the claims of Pequot control nearly to the Hudson, saying that a large part of the inhabitants of the country west of the Connecticut River became subject to the Mohawks, and that every year two old Mohawks might be seen going from village to village collecting tribute and issuing orders from the Great Council of the Five Nations at Onondaga.

For that matter they all seem to have been related, for according to Uncas' genealogy as given to the whites in 1679, Sassacus' grandmother was a daughter of the Chief Sachem of the Narragansetts, Uncas' mother was a sister of Sassacus' grandfather and Uncas himself married a daughter of Sassacus. So we see that Uncas the Mohican was of the royal house of the Pequots and married into the family, being a distant cousin and son-in-law of Sassacus, whose position he sought continuously to usurp; and finally, being so thoroughly despised by all the tribes of the federation except his own that he could accomplish nothing unaided, joined the English against his own people for the sole purpose of securing the overthrow of Sassacus and the Pequot tribe in order to place his own tribe with himself at its head in the dominant position in the league. That he would have betrayed the English with the same facility had the opportunity presented itself without danger to his precious scalp goes without saying.

The Chief Sachem of the Narragansetts, whose daughter Woipeguand the grandfather of Sassacus is said by Uncas to have married, was named Wekoum. This must have been the father or grandfather of Tashtussuch, unless the chieftaincy descended collaterally, and in that case either the uncle or great uncle. So we see that Wopigwooit, Sassacus and Uncas were cousins, a few degrees removed, of Canonicus and Miantonomo who were their most deadly foes.

Intermarriages between members of the ruling houses of the neighboring nations in intervals of peace would seem from this to have prevailed among the Indians just as it has among civilized peoples, but with no better results so far as it affected the peace of the nations.

English colonies having been established on the Connecticut River, in 1633 Sassacus began the series of depredations that terminated in the Pequot war. The first overt act was the murder of Captain Stone and his crew. Stone was a trader from Virginia, said to have been unscrupulous in his dealings and addicted to drunkenness, but this does not appear to have contributed to his misfortune, as the Indians did not complain of any mistreatment on his part when they made their defence for his murder, which does not appear to have been presented until 1636.

Between these dates the authorities had made a

treaty with Sassacus, and had succeeded in patching up some sort of a peace between him and the Narragansett Sachems. By the terms of this treaty, the Pequots were to pay to the whites four hundred fathoms of wampum for the Narragansetts for some damage occasioned by their depredations. In this connection it is of interest to note that we find mention of payments of wampum much more frequent in the dealings of the Pequots and Narragansetts than of any other tribes, and this bears out the statement of Bradford that the Indians about Plymouth and the Massachusetts had none or very little wampum, "only it was made and kepte amonge the Narigansets and Pequentes, which grew rich and potent by it."

The treaty to which I have referred, and which was expressly sought by Sassacus, who sent messengers to Boston to secure the friendship of the English, was made in 1634, but, in 1636, war broke out between the Pequots and the Narragansetts, and in the same year, the authorities charged Sassacus with having harbored some of the murderers of John Oldham, and with having failed to pay the wampum which he had agreed to pay by the terms of his treaty, and another six hundred fathoms was added to this by the authorities, probably as a penalty for harboring Oldham's murderers, although they do not appear to have been given any hearing on this charge; but this seems to have been the only fresh outrage against the whites or charged to the Pequots which would warrant the demand.

A fleet of small vessels was fitted out at Boston

to sail to the Pequot country to secure satisfaction or punish the offenders. John Endicott was placed in command, with Captain Underhill commanding the military force of ninety men. Endicott's instructions were to go first to Block Island and take possession of it in the name of the colony, to spare the women and children, but to put all the men to the sword in punishment for the murder of Oldham, although more than a dozen of them had already been slain by Gallop and his crew at the time of the discovery of the offence, and Canonicus had sent Miantonomo with two hundred men to punish them further.

From Block Island, Endicott was to proceed to the Pequot country, obtain the murderers of Stone and one thousand fathoms of wampum. It is worthy of note in this connection that Stone was murdered before the treaty between the Pequots and the English, so it seems like a stale demand to us at this remote time. He was also to demand some of their children as hostages and to take them by force if the demand was refused. At Block Island, Underhill reported the killing of fourteen natives and the wounding of others, but the Narragansetts claimed that they killed only one.

Arriving at Saybrook, Lieutenant Gardiner, the commander of the garrison, protested against the enterprise, saying, "You have come to raise a nest of wasps about our ears and then you will flee away." Events that followed showed Gardiner to be in the right. As the expedition sailed up the river the natives became much alarmed and called out to them from the shore inquiring if the English had come to kill them, to which Endicott replied that the Pequots or their allies had destroyed an English vessel and killed ten Englishmen on the river; that their sachem had agreed to surrender the murderers (this appears to be the first mention of any such agreement) but had not yet fulfilled his agreement, and that the English had now come for them, and, if the Pequots were wise, they would immediately give them up. They then demanded one thousand fathoms of wampum for the destruction of the English property and for their faithlessness in not observing the treaty. The Pequot ambassador tried to justify the killing of Stone by telling about an earlier expedition in which some whites (Dutch) had seized their sachem and demanded a ransom of a bushel of wampum; that they had promised to send the sachem ashore upon the collection of this wampum; that the Indians had collected the wampum and paid it to them and they then brought the sachem ashore dead. When Stone came, they did not know the difference between the Dutch and the English and did what they did to avenge their sachem's death.

Endicott refused to accept this explanation and persisted in his demand for the heads of those who had slain their people. Endicott's men accomplished nothing but the burning of wigwams, wasting the corn, and staving canoes, and then returned to Boston. This exasperated the Pequots to such an extent that they endeavored to induce the Narragansetts to join with them in a general uprising, as related by Miantonomo to Roger Williams. Massachusetts colonists, though having banished Williams because of his heterodox views, appealed to him to use his influence with the Narragansetts to prevent the culmination of this attempt, and, fortunately for the colonists, Williams succeeded, if indeed the Narragansetts seriously entertained the proposition.

The Pequots seem to have become actively hostile to the English from this time, attempting, as we have already seen, to secure the assistance of their constant enemies, the Narragansetts, in a general uprising, and, failing in this, they started in on their own account in the spring of 1637, by attacking Weathersfield and Saybrook.

These open acts of aggression aroused the Connecticut colonies, and their anxiety soon spread to those of Massachusetts. At Hartford on May 1, the general court adopted an order the beginning of which was as follows: "It is ordered that there shall be an offensive war against the Pequoitt, and that there shall 90 men be levied out of the three Plantacions, Harteford, Weathersfield and Windsor (vizt) out of Harteford 42, Windsor 30, Weathersfield 18, under comande of Captaine Jo. Mason." June 2, a second levy of thirty was made, as follows, "Harteford 14, Windsor 10, Weathersfield 6," and on June 26 still another of ten apportioned to "Harteford 5, Windsor 3, Weathersfield 2."

Massachusetts, alarmed by the disquieting reports brought in and sent in by Miantonomo, and the Saybrook and Weathersfield massacres, had started preparations even earlier than Connecticut, for on April 18, at a session of the General Court, a levy of one hundred and sixty men had been ordered, and the sum of six hundred pounds had been appropriated to meet the expenses. It was expressly provided that the forty men that "were lately sent to Saybrook" were to be accounted of said number. These forty were the men who made up the expedition sent to the Narragansett country to join Miantonomo's force as referred to in an earlier chapter.

Plymouth, on June 7, provided for raising thirty men for the land forces and as "many as necessary to man the barque," by voluntary enlistment. Forty men volunteered unconditionally and three more "if they should be prest."

Mason's orders were to sail down the Connecticut to Saybrook and attack the Pequot forts, of which there were two, from the west; but he decided to disobey the order and to attack from the east. His expedition left Hartford on May 10, and arrived in Narragansett Bay on the twentieth. The next day being the Sabbath they stayed on their boats. Tuesday they disembarked and Wednesday received word from Roger Williams of the arrival of forty men from Massachusetts under the command of Captain Patrick. Williams requested them to wait for this reënforcement; but, leaving thirteen men in charge of the boats, Mason pushed on with seventy-seven whites, sixty Mohicans and two hundred or more Narragansetts. The next morning they reached a fort of the Niantics twelve miles east of the Paucatuc River; and not being entirely

sure of the friendliness or even neutrality of Ninigret, the Niantic Sachem, they surrounded the fort.
Two hundred warriors from this tribe then joined
them and they started out, seventy-seven whites
and a motley gathering of five hundred Narragansetts, Niantics and Mohicans.

One writer of comparatively recent times, who
derives his information concerning the expedition
from Captain Mason, Trumbull and others, says
the start was made on June 5, but other historians
fix the date of the attack on the Pequot fort as
May 26, and we are naturally led to inquire why
Mason delayed so long after reaching and surrounding the Niantic fort. They left the place of debar-
kation on Wednesday, May 23, and arrived at the
Niantic fort the next morning, and it does not
appear that they were delayed there.

On arriving at the frontier the same writer tells
us some of the Narragansetts seemed to be seized
with fear and turned back, but Captain Mason
pressed on, and on halting for the night at a point
three miles west of the Paucatuc River, learned of
the location of the two forts of the Pequots, one of
which was on the Pequot or Niantic River and the
other on the Mystic. As the most westerly one
could not be reached before midnight, Mason decided to attack that on the Mystic first, and to camp
at Porter's Rocks, a short distance from the fort, the
following night and make an assault early in the
morning.

Their presence at Porter's Rocks was known to
the occupants of the fort, for at their last camp the

troops could plainly hear the Indians shouting their defiance. At three o'clock in the morning preparations for the attack were begun. There were two entrances to the fort, and the plan of assault involved the entrance of one of these by Captain Mason with a part of the force and the other by Captain Underhill with the remainder. Their Indian allies, having been encouraged or restrained from retreating only by Mason's urgent appeal to them to stay and see whether the English would fight or not, formed a circle far in the rear. It is related that Uncas was present in person at the attack and when asked how many of the Mohicans would run, replied, "all but me." (And this turned out to be true in a sense, for Mason says they all deserted except Uncas after the fight.)

Mason and Underhill reached their objectives at almost the same moment, and Underhill entered without opposition, but when Mason was within a few feet of his entrance the barking of a dog aroused the sentry who rushed back shouting, "Owanux, Owanux," the English, the English. The Indians were so panic-stricken by the suddenness of the attack that they offered very little effective resistance, the English immediately coming to close quarters and using swords as well as muskets. Mason ordered fire-brands applied to the seventy wigwams within the fortification, and in a very short time the work of destruction was complete, the whites forming a close inner circle, and the Indians an outer circle to stop any who succeeded in getting through the inner line. Captain Mason says between six and seven hundred Pequot warriors perished in this attack, one hundred and fifty having come from the other fort during the night; seven were captured and seven escaped. It is also said that three hundred came up from the other fort and attacked the English while on their way to the Pequot or Niantic River where they were to meet their vessels, but they kept them at bay until the arrival of the boats. Captain Patrick and his forty men were on the vessels, and twenty men from Massachusetts arrived in time to join in the attack on the fort. This accounts for the presence of Captain Underhill who was a Massachusetts man. Outside of these twenty, Mason had no active assistance in the assault, and the entire attacking party consisted of less than one hundred men, of whom two were killed and twenty wounded.

Mason then took up his march to Saybrook instead of returning by the boats, no doubt intending to complete the work he had so auspiciously begun, and gather in the remnants of the tribe. On the way to Saybrook they fell in with a "people called Nayanticks, belonging to the Pequots, who fled to a swamp for refuge." These were the western Niantics, the eastern branch of the tribe being the people whom Mason found east of the Paucatuc River, and some two hundred of whom joined him in the expedition.

Mason tells us that the remnant "fled into several parts toward Manhatance" (Manhattan?), and two hundred old men, women and children, who were found in a swamp near New Haven, gave themselves up, and the rest were finally rounded up in a swamp in Fairfield where they were completely surrounded; but about sixty or seventy broke through that part of the line held by Captain Patrick and escaped; and one hundred and eighty were captured.

DeForest says that in this flight they passed through the territory of the Hammonassetts, Quinipoigs and Wepauwags or Paugussetts, and of course they would of necessity cross the land of the western Niantics before coming to any of these.

The men who made this last stand must have been the occupants of the western fort, who made their escape after the disastrous defeat of their tribesmen at the Mystic fort. Sassacus himself was in the western fort, but abandoned his tribe and, with twenty men, including one of his brothers and at least five sachems, sought safety with the Mohawks, probably preferring to take chances with them, notwithstanding the fact that at some earlier time he had made war upon them, rather than face capture at the hands of the English and their Mohican and Narragansett allies, and the fate that he knew awaited him if taken by them. He may have thought that the Mohawks would extend to him in his humbled position the hospitality of a foeman to his fallen enemy. If such was his belief he miscalculated the Mohawk character, for they put him and all of his party except one named Minotto, who escaped by flight, to death and the following August they sent his scalp with that of his brother and five sachems to Hartford. It is claimed that

the Mohawks were induced to thus destroy the
party by bribes from the Narragansetts, but whatever may have been the impelling motive, it does
not speak very highly for the Mohawks. If they
did not wish to harbor them through a desire to
avoid conflict with the English, as neutrals they
might at least have allowed them to pass on or, at
the worst, have turned them over to the whites; not
that the latter course would have helped the Pequots, but it would have placed the responsibility
for their subsequent treatment where it belonged.

And so perished the great Pequot nation and Sassacus, its chief. Some historians speak of refugees
scattered here and there, and tell us that some of
them fled to Uncas and some even to their ancient
enemies, the eastern Niantics and Narragansetts;
and then go on to say that on October 1, 1638,
there were found to be two hundred men of them,
including the old and feeble and the young and
strong, who were divided as follows: eighty to Miantonomo, twenty to Ninigret and one hundred to
Uncas. They were prohibited from using the name
Pequot and were ordered to assume the name of the
tribe to which they were attached. That this order
was not strictly enforced appears from the fact that
in 1646 two small bodies of them had settled in their
old hunting grounds, one near the Thames and one
near the Paucatuc, where they were known by the
old name. The head of one of these groups was a
Pequot, and of the other, a nephew of Ninigret,
named Cushawashet, but more commonly called
Wequash Cook and Herman Garrett.

In 1655, the Commissioners of the United Colonies recognized these two bodies and appointed Garrett governor over the Paucatuc group and Cassassinimon governor of the other group, said then to be located near New London. This act of the commissioners was not pleasing to Uncas and he protested, but they refused to revoke the appointments, and instead conferred upon the two governors all royal privileges formerly belonging to sachems only.

Some historians vary the figures given above in writing of the distribution of the remnant of the tribe, and some speak of them as though they were not refugees, but those who surrendered at New Haven or were captured at Fairfield, and the question naturally arises, if they were not the captives so taken what did become of the latter? History does not leave us entirely in the dark on this point, however, as there is enough written to warrant the belief that they were distributed as slaves among the colonists, a fate that certainly befell the women, some of them being taken to Massachusetts, where, as we have already seen, one "little young squaw," said to be a daughter of Sassacus, was given to Sassamon for his services in the war, and afterwards became his wife. So these two hundred probably were the scattering refugees; but, if they were, a simple problem in addition gives us from ten to twelve hundred Pequot warriors, where Endicott saw three hundred, and DeForest thinks this was the total strength of the tribes, twenty-six in number, under Sassacus, or at least of as many of them

as were with him in this war. Unless these refugees
and the captives taken in the Fairfield swamp were
the same, there were three hundred and eighty, besides the sixty or seventy that escaped and the
twenty who fled with Sassacus, after the fight at the
Mystic fort.

My reason for saying that these two hundred who
were divided were probably actual refugees is that
there appears to have been some sort of treaty or
agreement between the whites and the Narragansetts, Niantics and Mohicans at the conclusion of
the war, by which the Indians bound themselves
not to harbor any Pequots, which would preclude
any prior distribution of the captives; and it is
worth noticing at this time that the only tribe that
lived up to this agreement was the Narragansetts
under Canonicus and Miantonomo, whom the whites
subsequently gave up to be murdered by the treacherous Uncas.

As early as July, 1637,—and this date lends color
to the belief that these two hundred were refugees
—the Massachusetts authorities had a quarrel with
Ninigret concerning the matter, and the Narragansetts told the authorities at Boston that Uncas
was protecting a large number of them; but before
taking up the matter of this revelation, I will refer
briefly to Captain Mason's account of the trouble
the Connecticut authorities had with Ninigret on
the same score. He says that some of the captives — mark the word! — settled at Paucatuc contrary to agreement, as claimed by the English; and
he was sent against them. When he arrived on the

scene he saw three hundred armed Indians across the river, having previously been attacked by Ninigret's warriors of whom he captured seven.

Otash, Miantonomo's brother, then came up and said they were Miantonomo's men. Ninigret's men were defiant, and, when told that the whites had come to destroy the Pequots because they had not kept their word, in that they were not to inhabit there, said the Pequots were good men and they would fight for them; they would fight Uncas but not the whites, who were spirits. Mason pressed on and destroyed crops and wigwams.

Among the Pequots harbored by Ninigret were two brothers of Sassacus, and a report that he was about to give his daughter in marriage to one of them subsequently caused the colonists some anxiety. There appear to be some inconsistencies in Mason's narrative as the men could not well have been Miantonomo's and Ninigret's unless the former had some greater authority over the latter than he seems to have exercised.

To return to Uncas; upon the defeat of the Pequots and the almost complete annihilation of the tribe, followed by the prohibition of the use of the name, the Mohicans became the dominant tribe in the federation and Uncas was their Sachem. DeForest says of him he "was selfish, jealous and tyrannical." He might have said a great deal more that is not generally considered complimentary, and still have been within bounds.

When Wopigwooit was slain by the Dutch, Uncas laid claim to the Great Chieftaincy, basing his claim on his own descent and strengthening it by the royal birth of his wife. He engaged in open war with Sassacus over the succession; but most of the tribes of the federation adhered to Sassacus, and Uncas was defeated and fled to the Narragansetts. This life of an exile apparently becoming irksome to him, he sent a humble message to Sassacus begging permission to return to his people. Sassacus, more magnanimous than wise in this respect, granted the desired permission on condition of submission and good behavior for the future. Uncas, with the duplicity, deceit and treachery which marked his entire career, promised to behave and came back to the Mohicans.

Apparently this was but the first step towards the accomplishment of a well-defined purpose to begin his plottings against Sassacus again, for in a short time he was once more a fugitive from his own domain. Again he was pardoned upon his submission and promise of good behavior, and again was compelled to flee. On each of these successive flights to the Narragansett country, some of his warriors remained, until finally his forces were so reduced by these losses that he was no longer dangerous, and he was again permitted to return, although deprived of all of his lands. He then devoted his entire attention to the hunt, in which two sons of a sister of Sassacus were his constant companions. These men, who, as will be seen by reference to Uncas' genealogy of the Chiefs of the Pequots, were cousins of his wife, afterwards quarreled with Sassacus and fled to the Narragansett country where they remained.

When the Narragansetts informed the authorities at Boston that Uncas was protecting many Pequot fugitives, that worthy came to Boston with a retinue of thirty-seven warriors, bringing a present of twenty fathoms of wampum for the governor, which he refused to receive unless some explanation was made of Uncas' conduct in giving assistance to the Pequots. When this refusal was communicated to him he was somewhat perplexed, but only for a moment, for, like the accomplished liar he was, he soon recovered his composure and solemnly assured the authorities that he had no Pequots and that all those who accompanied him were true Mohicans.

The authorities, taking him at his word, accepted his present; Uncas then placed his hand on his heart and addressed the governor in these words: "This heart is not mine. It is yours. I have no men; they are all yours. Command me any hard thing and I will do it. I will never believe any Indian's words against the English. If any Indian shall kill an Englishman, I will put him to death, be he ever so dear to me."

On their way back from Boston to their own country they passed Roger Williams' house; and one of their party, having become lame, stopped there. This man was named Wequanmugs, the son of a Narragansett father and a Mohican mother, and so, free to travel in the hunting grounds of both tribes. In a conversation with Mr. Williams he told him that Miantonomo had only two Pequots, both of whom had been captured by his warriors and were not voluntary refugees under his protection; that the

Niantics had about sixty under Wequash Cook, Ninigret's nephew, who, as we have already seen, under the name of Herman Garrett was later appointed governor over them with the dignity of Sachem.

Williams then inquired if there were any Pequots in the party that accompanied Uncas to Boston, to which he replied that there were six and gave their names, saying at the same time that two of them had slain Englishmen. Williams, who apparently had not the confidence in Uncas that the Massachusetts and Connecticut authorities always manifested, wrote down the names and sent them to Governor Winthrop with an account of his conversation with Wequanmugs. DeForest observes: "The revelation must have been peculiarly gratifying to Winthrop, as he had given to the sachem a fine red coat on his departure, and had defrayed his expenses while he remained in Boston, and furnished him with provision for his homeward journey, and dismissed him with a general letter of protection." This visit of Uncas to Boston was in July, 1638, three months before the distribution of the two hundred refugees, and while the original agreement between the whites and the Indians concerning the harboring of Pequots was in full force.

During the same summer that Uncas made this visit to Boston, some Pequots who had not submitted to or taken refuge with any other tribe, but had remained independent, sent some of their chief men to Hartford with an offer to give themselves up to the English if their lives might be spared.

Both Uncas and Miantonomo were thereupon summoned to Hartford to confer with the authorities concerning the disposition of this group, as well as to adjust certain disputes between themselves. Miantonomo set out with an imposing train composed of his wife and children, several of his sachems and not less than one hundred and fifty warriors. Roger Williams and two other Englishmen also accompanied him. Before reaching Hartford they were met by a number of Narragansetts returning to their own country from Connecticut, who complained that the Pequots and Mohicans had robbed them; and following close on the heels of this complaint came another from a Nipmuck clan, subject to the Narragansetts, that they had been plundered shortly before by a band of six or seven hundred Indians of these two tribes and their confederates. They reported that this band of marauders had spoiled twenty-three fields of corn and robbed three Narragansetts who were staying with the Nipmucks, and were then lying in wait for Miantonomo and his party; and they said that some of the band had threatened to boil Miantonomo in a kettle.

Miantonomo was not to be deterred by threats of this character and pressed on, reaching Hartford in safety, where he proceeded to lay before the Council these several causes of complaint. Uncas was not there, having sent a messenger to tell the authorities that he was too lame to attend. Haynes, one of the leading men in the Council, and later governor of the colony, said this was a very lame excuse, and sent messengers to request him to make his appearance. The urgency of this message seems to have proved a very effective liniment, for he recovered from his lameness at once and repaired to Hartford, bringing with him an Indian to testify that the party which had been in the Nipmuck country consisted of only one hundred and not six or seven, and that they took only a little corn for roasting and did a few other harmless things but no damage. This was flatly contradicted by the Narragansetts, but the Council was unable to decide where the truth lay and dismissed the charges.

This was one of the early instances of the leaning of the colonial authorities towards Uncas, to which I have called general attention in a preceding chapter, and of which I may have occasion to cite other instances. He had broken his promise concerning the harboring of Pequots. He had lied to Governor Winthrop about it. He had deliberately attempted to evade their request to come to Hartford for a conference with the Council and Miantonomo concerning the disposition of Pequots who had offered to give themselves up, and to discuss his own differences with Miantonomo, and when he did come finally on second and urgent request, brought one of his own followers as a witness to meet a charge that he did not know had been preferred, unless his own guilty knowledge of its truth was sufficient to make it certain that the charge would be made; and the word of this subject of his was taken as against that of the Narragansetts, and he was found not guilty.

The magistrates then attempted to effect a recon-

ciliation between the two sachems; and Miantonomo, although the party aggrieved by their
decision, entered into the spirit that prompted their
efforts, and, with the magnanimity that always
marked his character, twice invited Uncas to feast
with him on some venison which his hunters had
brought in. This invitation Uncas sullenly refused,
notwithstanding the urgent request of the magistrates that he accept.

Before leaving Hartford, Miantonomo, at a
private conference, gave the Council the names of
all the remaining members of the Pequot tribe who
had been guilty of killing Englishmen. A list of
these names was read to Uncas who admitted that
it was correct. Miantonomo then said that of the
remnants of the tribe Canonicus had none; he had
ten or eleven out of the seventy who had submitted
to him, the others never having come in, or having
returned to their old hunting grounds after coming
in; and the rest were either with the Mohicans or
in their ancient territory, which it will readily be
seen amounted to the same thing, as the Pequot
territory naturally became Mohican territory when
the last-named tribe gained the ascendency in the
federation. If there is any truth to the charge that
Miantonomo was jealous of the increase of Uncas'
power by the addition of the Pequots, we do not
need to look further for the reason. It was not because of the allotment of them to the several tribes,
but the fact that Uncas and Ninigret, who was the
sachem of a tribe that had been of the old Mohican
federation, though under Narragansett protection

and living on Narragansett territory, had almost all of them, no doubt through their own inducement to them to live in their territory; and Ninigret in the event of hostilities was just as likely to favor Uncas as he was to side with Miantonomo.

On the presentation of this last statement as to the then location of the remaining Pequots, to Uncas, he attempted to evade the question and the giving in of any account, saying that he did not know the names of his Pequots, that he had only twenty, but that Ninigret and three other Niantic sachems had many of them. He afterwards admitted that he had thirty, and was allowed ten days to bring in their names, and messengers were dispatched to the Niantic country to secure a list of the Pequots with them.

It was on the lists thus furnished that the allotment was made on October 1, 1638. From what we know of Uncas, it requires no great stretching of our credulity to believe that he might, at that very time, be protecting many more than he reported, and Miantonomo, knowing that this was likely to be the case, had another reason for fearing trouble on account of his double dealing and deceit, to say nothing of the tendency on the part of the colonial authorities to favor Uncas in all matters in controversy between them, which first manifested itself at the conference to which I have referred and which continued constantly to the end.

I have already called attention to the hostility of these two chiefs and of the complaints lodged with the authorities by Uncas against Miantonomo during the life of the latter, in the chapter devoted to the last-named chief, as well as to the culmination of the controversy between them by the death of Miantonomo on Sachem's Plain; and without repeating, I will now proceed to a brief recital of some of the principal events in which Uncas figured after he had secured the colonists' consent to the cold-blooded murder of his rival.

His troubles did not cease upon the removal of Miantonomo, but rather seemed to increase, the first fresh outbreak resulting from the claim of the Narragansetts that he had agreed to release their chief upon payment of a ransom, a part of which had been paid when the jealous Mohican, with his usual treachery, put him to death. We have seen that the authorities decided this case in favor of Uncas, but from what has already appeared concerning the character of that chief and of his machinations and the tendency of the whites to favor him, it is not difficult for us to believe that this was one of those judgments based upon policy rather than sound reasoning, with which the history of that period abounds.

In the fall of 1646, Herman Garrett, who, as we have seen, had established himself at the head of a group of Pequots west of the Paucatuc River, complained that Uncas and three hundred of his warriors had attacked one of their hunting parties and plundered them. Upon being summoned to Court on this complaint, Uncas admitted that he had done wrong in committing this act of violence in such close proximity to the English settlement, but attempted to palliate the offence by a counter charge that Garrett's men had hunted on Mohican grounds without leave.

Before Uncas could get away from New Haven, where this complaint was heard, William Morton of New London came forward with another charge. Accompanied by three Pequots, Morton came in and related a startling story told to him by one of the Pequots who came with him, in which this man, whose name was Wampushet, said Uncas had hired him and two Pequot powwows for fifteen fathoms of wampum to wound another Indian and then charge the crime upon Garrett.

Wampushet was then called before the Council, and denied the story he had told to Morton, but not that he had told it; and then proceeded to charge the entire plot to Garrett, just as he had told Morton it was originally planned. They were unable to shake him in his last version, and as there was no evidence against Uncas except what Wampushet had previously told Morton and now stoutly denied, the complaint was dismissed. Morton and the other Pequots who came in with him declared that Uncas must have hired Wampushet to change his testimony, and this plot so closely resembles the one revealed to the Massachusetts authorities, and disbelieved by them, at the time when Uncas claimed to have been shot through the arm with an arrow, that we are quite naturally led to inquire whether this was not actually one of the means employed by Uncas to rid himself of rivals or enemies whom he feared or whose power he desired to curb, with the assistance of the English.

In this last cited case, in order to obtain a clear view of the situation, it must be borne in mind that Garrett was a Niantic, and a nephew of the sachem of that tribe; the group over whom he had established himself were living on old Pequot territory, and if suspicion could be fastened on Garrett, it would naturally reflect upon the Niantics, and this group of Pequots would naturally be given to Uncas by the English.

It was not long after this last affair that forty-eight Pequots presented themselves before the Council. They said they had not fought against the whites, having fled the country when the war broke out, and presumably returned to their old hunting grounds after its conclusion. They complained that Uncas had taken away their wives, robbed them of their corn and beans, spoiled their nets and extorted wampum from them. Uncas did not appear in person to answer to this charge, but sent Foxon, his Chief Counsellor, who either pretended ignorance, or attempted to palliate the offences.

John Winthrop was the next complainant on behalf of a group of Indians, who charged Uncas and his brother Wawequa with having attacked this group with one hundred warriors, plundered the people and carried away their cattle, wampum, bear skins, beaver skins and other articles of value. Foxon admitted this attack, but excused Uncas, by saying that he had not personally had any part in it, and knew nothing about it, being away at New

Haven, and had not participated in the spoils. At this same time a complaint was also made against him for having gone over to Fisher's Island and broken two canoes, frightened an Indian and plundered the island.

The great solicitude of the magistrates for this precious cut-throat is shown by the penalty imposed upon him for these three outrages. He was ordered to pay a fine of one hundred fathoms of wampum when the Pequots returned to him. The Pequots, being the forty-eight who complained of his maltreatment of them, never returned, as the magistrates must have foreseen, and so he escaped scot free.

About 1649 or 1650, he appears to have had a real grievance; for there seems no good reason to doubt that he was actually attacked while on board an English vessel, by Cataquin, a Narragansett, who wounded him in the breast with a sword so seriously that he came very near putting an end to complaints both by and against the fawning Mohican.

Ninigret was charged with being the instigator of this plot, and Pessacus was alleged to have been implicated in it. Nothing appears to have been pressed against the latter, but Ninigret went to Boston where he attempted to clear himself by a counter charge that the Mohicans had carried this story; but was reminded that Cataquin had told it to Captain Mason and others when he surrendered to the Mohicans. They let Ninigret off with a sharp reprimand and warning of what was likely to happen to him if he persisted in his plotting. At the same time they sent word to Uncas, who was recovering from his wound, that Cataquin was at his disposal, and there the historians leave the matter, probably assuming that the intelligent reader of Uncas' life and character does not need to be told what happened to Cataquin.

But the colonial authorities were not yet rid of this pestiferous scoundrel, for, in 1653, he again sprang into the lime light with a complaint to Haynes, who had then become governor, that the Narragansetts and Niantics were attempting to organize an expedition against him at New Netherlands; and he related with great detail how Ninigret had been to Manhattan, where he had received a large box of powder and bullets in exchange for a large quantity of wampum, and had then attended a council of Indians from the Hudson River in an endeavor to secure their assistance in a contemplated attack upon Uncas and the English. How much of this had a foundation in fact, and how much was the product of Uncas' suspicion and jealousy is not established. There seems to be no doubt that Ninigret did make a trip to the Hudson at about that time, but it was never shown that it was for any other purpose than that of legitimate trade.

At this same sitting of the Court, Uncas also complained that Ninigret had sent a present of wampum to a "Monheag Sachem," asking him to send men skilful in magic and poison and promising one hundred fathoms more of wampum upon the poisoner's return after the accomplishment of the

purpose for which he was wanted. Uncas claimed
to have intercepted the canoe which was bringing
the party, which consisted of the conjurer and six
other persons, one of whom was a Pequot and the
rest Narragansetts; he said that Wampeag, one of
the Narragansetts, had confessed the entire plot and
pointed out the "Monheag" who had been sent to
carry it out, whereupon the Mohicans had fallen
upon the alleged poisoner in a rage and put him to
death.

This was the fourth alleged attempt upon the life
of Uncas, and every one of them implicated some
rival whose power he feared, and whom he desired
to remove with the aid of the English. They all
savor so much of the craftiness and cunning for
which he was so notorious, and as there is direct evidence that at least some of them were framed by
Uncas himself, to say nothing of the strong chain of
circumstantial evidence leading to the same conclusion, we are led to doubt whether there was any
real foundation for any of them except the attack
by Cataquin.

On the other hand, the authenticity of this attempt seems to be sufficiently well established to
give rise to the question whether there may really
not have been something in some of the other
charges. That the English did not give full faith
and credit to them is apparent from the fact that
they did nothing with respect to two of them.
Whatever may have been the facts, we are inevitably forced to the conclusion that Uncas was either
a wily schemer constantly striving to increase his

power by preferring against his rivals charges based
upon suspicion or framed by him; or that his
enemies really did make the attempts with a view
to ridding the world of the most selfish, treacherous
and unscrupulous scoundrel produced by the Indians of New England during the period covered by
our knowledge of them. That he was thoroughly
despised by all the other sachems of southern New
England goes without saying, and their hatred of
him is to their credit. He was as thoroughly hated
as his early rival, Miantonomo, was loved and respected.

Puffed up with the favors the English showed
him, and their apparent readiness to lend themselves to the furtherance of his schemes by deciding always in his favor whenever any issue between
him and other Indians was presented, and letting
him off without even a reprimand when he offered
no defence to his outrages,—in 1661 he attacked
the Indians at Quabaug in western Massachusetts,
and killed some and took others prisoners. These
Indians were of a Nipmuck tribe subject to Massasoit, and the Massachusetts colonial authorities, in
pursuance of their treaty obligations to that chief,
sent word to Uncas, demanding the release of the
prisoners. Receiving no reply, they then arranged
with Captain Mason, who for twenty-five years had
been on friendly terms with Uncas, to repeat the
demand.

Upon Mason's arrival, Uncas at first excused
himself by saying that he had received the demand
from Massachusetts only twenty days before; and

said he did not know the Quabaugs were under the protection of the English; and then denied that they belonged to Ousamequim; saying they were subjects of a deadly enemy of the Mohicans named Onopequin; and, apparently not satisfied with these two defences, he next attempted to justify his act on the assumption that they were Ousamequin's men, by saying that the latter had repeatedly waged war upon the Mohicans as had his eldest son Wamsutta or Alexander. To cover his entire line of defence, he then assured them that, notwithstanding all these things, he had set the men free, although one of them was his own cousin, and had on several occasions taken up arms against him.

It will be difficult to find a more shifty and thoroughly truckling defence in the pages of history, and on which part of it the commissioners relied we are not told; and it may be that they did not believe any of it, but were content to keep him groveling to them. In any event, they seem to have accepted his excuse, and not to have required him to give satisfaction. Upon his defence being laid before Wamsutta, who was at Plymouth at the time, he contradicted Uncas' statement concerning the Quabaugs and said that they were his father's people, and that he had made war on Uncas only because of wrongs he had done them.

Without attempting to cover all his activities, I have called attention to enough to show his character. DeForest says: "It is not difficult to see why Uncas was forever at sword's points with sachems and tribes of his own race. His nature was mean and jealous and he was tyrannical. He was treacherous to his own people. He would accuse before the English some one or another as being too dangerous or treacherous. He was the unscrupulous ally of the English, obeying every nod and sign with which they favored him and took every advantage which they allowed, over his brethren of the forest. He accused Miantonomo, put him to death, oppressed the valiant Pequots, tracked Sequassen from his place of refuge among the Pecoupans and surrendered him to the colonists' magistrates, and finally complained to the English about Pessacus, Ninegret, of Mexam, of Mohansick, and of any sachem from whom he could possibly have anything to fear."

And this was the man whom the English backed against their faithful friend, who stood before them as a man, and not a slave, who protected them without doing injustice to others, and of whose sad fate DeForest writes: "Such was the end of Miantonomo, a sachem who seems to have been respected and loved by every one who was not fearful of his power."

In spite of his truckling to the English, and running to them with complaints, and in spite of all the favors he had received at their hands, they knew him well enough not to trust him at the outbreak of King Philip's war; and required him to give hostages for his good conduct; and he sent in two of his own sons, brothers of Oweneco, his eldest son, who was then the war chief of the nation; and they appear to have remained with the English throughout the war. Oweneco with two hundred of his warriors fought with the colonial armies at the Swamp Fight at Kingston, Rhode Island, on December 19, 1675, when fifty-one of them were killed and eighty-two wounded.

The Mohicans and Pequots also participated in other engagements, fighting with the colonists against the Wampanoags and Narragansetts, their ancient enemies, prompted, no doubt, by a desire to secure the overthrow of every other sachem of any importance and set themselves up as the dominant Indian power in southern New England upheld by English forces. It would seem from our study of the character of Uncas, that this was a sufficient guaranty against any misconduct on his part, but the men who knew him were not content even with this, but demanded further surety, a sad commentary on their confidence in the man they had upheld for nearly half a century.

In King Philip's war a few Nipmuck tribes and the Podunks joined King Philip; the other tribes of Connecticut remained neutral, except the western Niantics who seem to have come under the domination of Uncas upon the passing of the control of the nation from Sassacus to him.

The Niantics, who have been frequently referred to in this and in preceding chapters, appear to have been a tribe of the old Mohican federation, into which the Pequot invasion drove a wedge, forcing a part of them to the west and a part to the east, by reason of which they are sometimes referred to as the Eastern Niantics and the Western Niantics, and I have followed this classification in this chapter. I have referred to the location of the two branches. The western group seem to have been under complete domination of the Pequots and later of the Mohicans, and play no particular part in the early struggles between the various tribes or between them and the whites. That their sympathies were with Sassacus, and that they held a fort as a sort of second line of defence in the Pequot war seems fairly well established, and that they followed Uncas in the final struggle of the red and white races for the control of southern New England is certain. The Eastern Niantics maintained an independent position east of the Paucatuc, although under the protection of the Narragansetts, with whom they were so closely allied that some writers speak of them as Narragansetts. Their history is so mingled with that of the Narragansetts, Pequots and Mohicans and their activities have been so often referred to in these connections that they do not call for further comment here, except to call attention to the fact that, under their old sachem Ninigret, who had caused a vast amount of trouble up to 1654, they joined the whites against their race in the last great attempt to shake off the ever increasing fetters which the men they had befriended were constantly forging for their feet. In this war Ninigret's daughter Magnus, the "Old Queen of the Narragansetts," who was then the widow of Miantonomo's brother, followed the fortunes of King Philip.

Ninigret was a shrewd old observer of events,

and perhaps foresaw the outcome of the struggle and the futility of throwing his warriors into the "deadly breach" against the whites, and hoped to secure for his people some favorable consideration at the hands of the men whose progress he saw no chance of stopping. He fell into complete disfavor with the whites in 1654, and his power was broken, and with it no doubt his spirit. That his hope of perpetuating his race by aiding the English, like Uncas' dream of an Indian Empire within or beside a white, was without foundation, appeared in the sequel, for friend and foe have alike been swept away.

Uncas died in 1682 or 1683, and was succeeded by his son Oweneco, sometimes written Oneco, who was the war chief of the nation during the war. Oneco's son Cæsar succeeded him, and upon the death of Cæsar, Uncas' youngest son Ben seized upon the chieftaincy, and he was succeeded by his son Ben, the last of the Mohican sachems. So it will be seen that the second generation after Uncas saw his race despoiled of all the prerogatives of royalty, if, indeed, he and his descendants from the time he first began to run to the English with his complaints were anything more than mere tools in their hands to preserve order, or assist them in preserving order, among the Indians for the Englishmen's own ends.

The first Ben Uncas, according to his father's own statement, was illegitimate, Uncas saying of him that he was half dog, the mother being a poor beggarly squaw, not his wife. It was generally understood, however, both among the English and

Indians, that Ben's mother was a daughter of Foxon, Uncas' Chief Counsellor.

Two hundred years after Uncas began his plotting to establish a great Mohican nation, with himself as its ruler, all that remained of his dreams was a reservation of twenty-three hundred acres, four hundred and sixty of which were actually cultivated by about sixty descendants of the warriors who, under the leadership of Oweneco, aided the whites in their work of exterminating their own race. About an equal number was then scattered to all the points of the compass, and of all the one hundred and twenty or one hundred and twenty-five not more than twenty-five or thirty were of pure Mohican blood. One of these one hundred and twenty or twenty-five was Esther Cooper, a lineal descendant of Uncas, and so far as known the last of his race. This refers to 1849, and the figures are taken from DeForest's *History of the Connecticut Indians.*

Thus faded the dream of the ambitious, unscrupulous, lying and treacherous Uncas, who sought by subterfuge and treachery to grasp the sceptre of Empire from all the New England Indians, and died, as he lived, despised by the men for whose favor he sold his birthright and betrayed his countrymen. If Indian character depended upon him and such as he, we would have no difficulty in agreeing with the appraisals usually made of it, but, fortunately for the memory of the race, it has produced not only an Uncas, but a Massasoit, a Miantonomo and a Pometacom, whose heroic deeds save it from oblivion, or disgrace.

XI

KING PHILIP AND HIS CAPTAINS

THREE histories of King Philip's war were
written by men who lived through that peril-
ous period, and who ought, therefore, to know
whereof they write. The first of these to make its
appearance was by Rev. William Hubbard of Connecticut, and was published immediately after the
close of the war; the second was by Rev. Increase
Mather of Massachusetts, and consisted principally
of a repetition of what Hubbard had written without giving any credit to the earlier writer. This
work appeared in 1676 and is entitled *Magnalia*.
Just what the author means by the title is not
quite clear; but if the first part of it is from the
Latin *Magnus* (great), it is most appropriately
named, for of all the colossal monuments to cant
and bigotry erected in an age when cant and bigotry
seemed to count for religious fervor, this is easily
Magnalia, the greatest of them all. The third
was written by Thomas Church, a son of Captain
Benjamin Church, at his dictation, and from notes
made, as he says, at the time. This was published
in 1716, and ran through several editions. Captain
Church was in a position to know as much about the
war as any man of that time, and, consequently in a

position to know more than any man of other times. The principal difficulty with his work is the air of braggadocio running through it, the tendency to exaggerate the ego. In fact, the entire work reads more like the boasting of his prowess by an old man than an attempt to set down historical facts with an eye single to absolute accuracy, and justice to the character of his opponents. While we are obliged to resort, in a large measure, to these three works for our facts, the beauty of all of them is sadly marred, the first two by the narrowness and spleen of the writers, and the last by the spirit of self-aggrandizement that permeates it. But we are not left entirely to the accuracy and judgment of these three men. Fortunately for the memory of the Indians, another contemporary writer, before the conclusion of the war, set down some observations of his own, without spleen or prejudice, and without boasting. John Easton came to New England in 1634, and settled at Ipswich in the Massachusetts Bay Colony. Being a Quaker, he was soon forced to flee to Rhode Island to escape the penalties imposed by the Puritans of Massachusetts upon men who did their own thinking in religious matters, and whose thoughts did not coincide with those laid down by the men in authority, who assumed the prerogative of thinking for others as well as for themselves. He settled at Newport, Rhode Island, in 1638, and very soon arose to prominence, being governor's assistant in 1640 and 1643, and from 1650 to 1652; and in 1654, he was president under the first colonial charter, and governor of Rhode Island from 1672 to 1674. In speaking of him as governor of Rhode Island, the latter must not be confused with the Providence Plantations of Roger Williams, as Rhode Island in those days meant the Indian island of Aquidnick, the Rhode or Red Island of the English.

Governor Easton died before the war was concluded, but not without having written down some facts which it is well to keep in mind in connection with the history of that period; and which so incensed the Reverend Increase Mather that he tells us he hastened his work on account of it, apparently fearing that the truth would not reflect any particular credit upon the English at Plymouth; and so must be completely buried in a mass of misrepresentation, cant and bigotry. Unfortunately for himself and his so-called history, he manifests so much spleen throughout the work that the careful reader sees in it, not the righteous indignation of one who is unjustly accused, but the boiling rage of the criminal who is caught with the goods in his possession.

Governor Easton's history contains some information concerning the complaints of the Indians as related by themselves that throw such an interesting side light upon the beginning of King Philip's war that I am constrained to quote from it at length, simply changing the quaint spelling and applying modern rules of punctuation, to make the whole more easily intelligible. He says: "But for four years' time, reports and jealousies of war had been very frequent. Yet we did not think that now the war was breaking forth; but about a week before it did, we had cause to think it would. Then, to endeavor to prevent it, we sent a man to Philip that, if he would come to the ferry, we would come over to speak with him. About four miles we had to come; thither our messenger come to them; they, not aware of it, behaved themselves as furious, but suddenly appeased when they understood who he was and what he came for; he called his council and agreed to come to us; came himself unarmed and about forty of his men, armed. Then five of us went over; three were magistrates. We sat very friendly together. We told him our business, so to endeavor that they might not receive or do wrong. They said that was well; they had done no wrong, the English had wronged them. We said we knew the English said the Indians wronged them, and the Indians said the English wronged them, but our desire was the quarrel might rightly be decided in the best way, and not as dogs decided their quarrels. The Indians owned that fighting was the worst way; they then propounded how right might take place. We said by arbitration. They said that all English agreed against them, and so by arbitration they had much wrong; many miles square of land was taken from them, for the English would have English arbitrators; and unless they were persuaded to give in their arms, that thereby jealousy might be removed; and the English, having their arms, would not deliver them as they had promised until they consented to pay one hundred pounds; and now they had not so much sum or money; they

were as good be killed as leave all their livelihood.
We said they might choose a Indian king, and the
English might choose the Governor of New York,
that neither had case to say either were parties in
the difference. They said they had not heard of
that way and said we honestly spoke; so that we
were persuaded, if that way had been tendered, they
would have accepted. We did endeavor not to hear
their complaints, said it was not convenient for us
now to consider of, but to endeavor to prevent
war. . . . We knew what their complaints would
be; and, in our colony, had removed some of them
in sending for Indian rulers in what the crime concerned Indians lives, which they very lovingly accepted, and agreed to their execution, and said so
they were able to satisfy their subjects when they
knew an Indian suffered duly; but said in what
was only between their Indians, and not any town-
ships that we purchased, they would not have us
prosecute, and that they had a great fear to have
any of their Indians should be called or forced to
be Christian Indians. They said that such were in
everything more mischievous, only dissemblers, and
then the English made them insubject to their kings
and by their lying wronged their king. We knew it
to be true. . . . But Philip judged it to be dis-
honesty in us to put off the hearing any just complaint; therefore we consented to hear them. They
said they had been the first in doing good to the
English and the English the first in doing wrong;
said when the English first came, their king's father
was as a great man and the English as a little child;

he constrained other Indians from wronging the English, gave them corn and showed them how to plant; and was free to do them any good, and had let them have a hundred times more land then now the king had for his own people. But their king's brother, when he was king, came miserably to die, being forced to court, as they judged, poisoned. And another grievance was, if twenty of their honest Indians testified that an Englishman had done them wrong, it was as nothing; but if but one of their worst Indians testified against any Indian or their king, when it pleased the English, it was sufficient.

"Another grievance was when their kings sold land, the English would say it was more than they agreed to. And a writing must be proved against all them, and some of their kings had done wrong to sell so much. He loved his people not; and some being given to drunkenness, the English made them drunk and then cheated them in bargains; but no doubt their kings were forewarned not to part with their land for nothing, in comparison to the value thereof. Now, whom the English have owned for king or queen, they were disinherited, and make another king that would give or sell them these lands; that now they had no hopes left to keep any land.

"Another grievance, the English cattle and horses still increased; that when they removed thirty miles from where the English had anything to do, they could not keep their corn from being spoiled, they never being used to fence; and that when the English bought land of them, they would have kept their cattle upon their own land.

"Another grievance, the English were so eager to sell the Indians liquors that most of the Indians spent in drunkenness and *reneved* [probably reneged, in the sense of shifting the responsibility] upon the sober Indians, and they did believe even did hurt the English cattle; but their king could not prevent it.

"We knew that these were their grand complaints, but we only endeavored to persuade that all complaints be righted without war; but come for no other answer but that they had not heard of that way, for the governor of York and an Indian king to have a hearing of it. We had case to think, if it had been tendered, it would have been accepted. We endeavored that, however, they should lay down the war, for the English were too strong for them; they said then the English should do to them as they did when they were too strong for the English. So we departed without any discourteousness, and suddenly had letter from Plymouth Governor, they intended in arms to conform Philip, but no information what it was they required or what terms he refused to have their quarrel decided at, and in a week's time after we had been with the Indians, thus begun." He then proceeds to give an account of the first acts of hostilities, as related by all the historians of that date.

The unreliability of Reverend Increase Mather's account of the war may perhaps be fairly judged by his reflection upon this simple statement of facts made by a man who had no occasion or incentive to tell anything but the truth, and who related only his own experiences; as well as by Mather's attempt to discredit another narrative of the war written as he says "by a merchant of Boston," and published in London, of which the reverend writer says, "abounding mistakes therein caused me to think it necessary that a true history of this affair should be published." Continuing he says, "Whilst I was doing this, there came to my hands another narrative of this war written by a Quaker in Road Island, who pretends to know the truth of things, but that narrative being fraught with worst things than meer mistakes, I was thereby quickened to expedite what I had in hand." This undoubtedly refers to Easton's history, as no other narrative written by a Quaker in Rhode Island is known to exist.

Disregarding Church's apparent egotism, which really is not sufficient cause for doubting the truthfulness of his narrative, except perhaps, those portions of it which refer to his own exploits, writers of later date have drawn largely upon his record of events for their facts concerning the occurrences of the war, and, in a large measure, for information about the Indian chiefs who participated in it; and for the purposes of this work, I will follow their example, first calling attention to the fact that I do not propose to give even a résumé of the history of the war; but rather to confine myself to a brief consideration of the causes which led up to it, and to references to some of the men who joined with Philip in an attempt to shake off the shackles which the English had been systematically fastening upon them almost from the moment of the first interview between Massasoit and Governor Carver at Plymouth.

I have said that Major Winslow's forcible arrest of Wamsutta at Munponset Pond was the beginning of King Philip's war, and in a sense this is true, for, while the grievances which he and his counsellors enumerated to Governor Easton, and the acts of the English of which they then complained, had extended over a long period, this was the first open act of hostility.

Wamsutta had never subjected himself or his people to the authority of the colonists, and was not under their jurisdiction. He was an independent ruler, bound, it is true, by the obligations of whatever treaties he had entered into with the whites, as well as those entered into by his predecessor in behalf of his people, and answerable for violations of those obligations, as one people or nation is answerable to another under similar circumstances; but the Plymouth authorities had no more right, either legal or moral, to send an armed force into his territory to arrest him at the point of a pistol, than the duly constituted authorities of the United States would have to send an army into Mexico to arrest its president and bring him to Washington to render an account of alleged acts in violation of some agreement between the two countries. Such an act would be an act of war in the latter case, and it was an act of war in Wamsutta's case.

If the English chose to look upon his alleged conduct as a cause of war, and took this course of commencing hostilities "without denouncing any war," as Bradford complains that Miantonomo had done in his invasion of the Mohican territory eighteen years before, they have no reason to criticize the Indians for treating it as an act of open hostility. They had no definite evidence of any wrongdoing on the part of Wamsutta. Suspicions there were, and suspicions there had been from the very beginning; but they had usually turned out to be the product of the imagination or the outgrowth of the machinations of some wily chief to cast suspicion upon some rival whom he feared, and for whose overthrow he wished to enlist the assistance of the whites.

There were rumors that Wamsutta was trying to stir up trouble, to organize a general uprising. Where the rumors came from no one knows, but Wamsutta is said to have attributed it to some of the Narragansetts when Captain Willett went to Mount Hope to investigate; yet when the day arrived on which he was to attend Court at Plymouth, he was visiting in the Narragansett country. If any of the chiefs of that tribe were endeavoring to injure him in the eyes of the whites, he evidently still retained the friendship of some of them. The expression "stir up trouble and organize a general uprising" is capable of so many constructions, that we are left in the dark as to what he was suspected of doing. It is a sort of blanket indictment calculated to cover almost anything that the English might consider inimical to their interests.

If he went over to the Narragansett country to confer with the sachems of that federation concerning the encroachments of the English, to talk about his grievances, to discuss, in a perfectly proper manner, some method of securing concerted action in peaceably resisting further encroachments, it would be a stirring up of trouble, the organizing of a general uprising, even though there was no thought of war, because it might cause some trouble to the English in their land grabbing schemes. Besides, there is not a scrap of evidence produced to show that Wamsutta did even any of these things.

The whole story was probably without foundation; for had any such attempt been made, his counsellors would have known of it; and, being privy to it, and in close touch with his negotiations and arrangements, his arrest and death under such circumstances as surrounded them, circumstances that led his people to believe that he had been poisoned, as they claimed thirteen years later, was all that was needed to kindle the spark he is charged with having laid, into flame.

Notwithstanding this attack upon the person of his brother and upon the sovereignty of his people, Pometacom, or King Philip, seems at first to have been desirous of continuing the friendly relations with the whites that had marked the forty years of his father's reign after the signing of the treaty with Governor Carver. Within a very few months of his succession to the great chieftaincy, he renewed the covenant which Massasoit had made with the colonists; and in the winter of 1663–64 he sent to John Eliot for "books to learn to read and to pray unto God." What an opportunity was thus presented to the English to perpetuate the bonds of friendship that had existed between them and the Wampanoags from the beginning! Oh, for the hand of a Roger Williams or the Quaker Governor of Rhode Island at the helm for an hour at that time! The history of King Philip's war would never have been written if the Massachusetts colonies had adopted the Rhode Island and Providence method of dealing with the natives.

Many causes have been assigned for the outbreak that finally came, of which the one most frequently mentioned is the land question; and while it is undoubtedly true that the natives saw with alarm their forests cut down, their hunting grounds given over to the plow and to the pasturage of roving herds of cattle, and themselves constantly restricted to narrower and narrower limits, this was only one of the many causes as fully appears from the complaint which Philip presented to Governor Easton. The colonists say they never took an acre of the Indians' land except by purchase, and if taking advantage of the Indians' simplicity and lack of appreciation of the effect of their acts to secure a township for a red coat, a county for thirty-five pounds, can be dignified with the name of purchase, their claim is well founded. At the prices they paid, the five hundred and forty pounds received by Hunt for the twenty-seven natives carried away from Plymouth in 1614 would have purchased the whole of Massachusetts. The Indians had been crowded to the limit. Their sachems had improvidently parted with the land which was a necessity to the continued existence of their people, and there had resulted disputes as to what was sold, and "a writing must be proved against all them," a paper prepared by whom? and understood by whom? Not satisfied with thus driving sharp and unscrupulous bargains until only a small portion of the land where they had formerly roamed and hunted at will remained to the Indians, the whites, still coveting the few acres that were left to them, continued their acts of depredation until, goaded to desperation, with justice denied him, with his sovereign rights invaded, with no alternative left to him but to die a death of slow starvation, or the glorious death of a warrior fighting for his home and patrimony, the red man chose the latter.

The land difficulties undoubtedly first arose over the difference between the English and the Indian tenures. Individual allotments and individual ownership was an established principle of the English law, and while the colonists, after a while, forbade the purchase of land by individual whites from the Indians, except with the consent of the authorities, this did not stop the abuses that had arisen, for it does not appear that they ever vetoed a sharp bargain driven by one of their people with an Indian chief. Opposed to this idea of private ownership was the Indian tenure by which the title to the land was in the tribe, and the right to its use was a common right, as indeed the fruits of the soil and the spoils of the hunt were the common property of all, except that the hunter was allowed the skins of the animals killed by himself so far as the same were necessary to the embellishment and comfort of his wigwam and the clothing of himself and his family.

With this communistic idea thoroughly established in the Indian customs and laws, it is not surprising that they should have thought that their deeds were simply grants of rights to occupy in common with themselves; and they discovered the full import of their act only when the purchasers took steps to dispossess them entirely; and it was thus that the natives said the English claimed more than they had granted and "there must be a writing," and when disputes arose "the English would have an English arbitrator," and the decision was, of course, always against the Indian.

The course pursued by the English in their dealings with the natives, coupled with the lack of skill in driving bargains on the part of the latter, who were induced in some way to put their marks to papers the true import of which they no more understood than they did the mystery of their existence and the wonders of nature, for a bauble which was soon gone, was gradually reducing them to a virtual state of vassalage to the men whom they had welcomed, and with whom they were willing to share their possessions, but who were not satisfied to share, and seized upon every opportunity to grasp the whole. In fact, their treatment of Wamsutta is evidence that the English had already assumed the authority to look upon them as vassals.

When a proud and independent people awake to the fact that this is their fate, but two courses are open to them, either complete submission by active consent or by silent acquiescence; or armed resistance. The Mohicans, Pequots and Niantics chose submission by active consent, the other Connecticut Indians, except the Podunks and a few Nipmucks, submission by tacit non-resistance; and the Wampanoags, the Narragansetts, the Podunks and most of the Nipmucks in Massachusetts and the few mentioned in Connecticut, chose armed resistance; and all met the same fate. The resisting warriors merely hastened theirs, preferring the death of warriors amid the shouts of battle in the deadly breach, to the death by slow starvation with their livelihood gone, or the living death of vassalage. Annihilation was the doom that was written for them in every scrap of paper to which they put their marks. Native simplicity, relying upon the native code of honor and native customs, could not stand before European greed. What seemed to Massasoit and to others following in his footsteps to be the path of wisdom, viewed in the light he possessed, turned out to be the path of destruction for his people. The burning embers from the peace pipe he extended to the first settlers kindled into a flame that enveloped and wiped out his race.

So while the act of Major Winslow was the first overt act in the great war, the causes that led up to it had existed for a long time, reaching back at least to the unjustified murder of Miantonomo in 1643, an act which was undoubtedly an important factor in deciding the course of the Narragansetts; but while the acts of which the Indians complained had continued over a long period, it apparently took the simple natives a long time to grasp their full import, and still Philip was willing to continue the chain of friendship until he became convinced, by fresh encroachments and continued acts of aggression and abuse, that the two races with their different customs of living and different codes of honor could not coexist on the same soil. Then resulted the war of extermination for one or the other.

That this war was not necessary we now know; that all that was required to prevent it was fair play and simple justice on the part of the whites, no one who reads the history of those times without passion or prejudice will attempt to gainsay. The issue of the war resulted in the establishment of the ideals of government and the freedom we cherish, but the same results might have been secured without the stain upon the white man's escutcheon that time can never efface.

In justice to the colonial authorities it ought to be said that not all the acts complained of should be laid directly at their doors; but while undoubtedly many of them were committed without authority, and not in pursuit of any general policy, the commissioners and magistrates cannot fully escape the responsibility for them, because when offences against the Indians were called to their attention they did nothing to correct the abuses. That they had no confidence in some of their own people in their dealings with the natives is clearly shown by a letter written to Governor Bradford by Robert Cushman as early as 1623, in which the writer says: "In the mean space know these things, and I pray you be advised a little. Mr. Weston hath quite broken off from our company through some discontents that arose betwixt him and some of our adventurers, and hath sould all his adventures, and hath now sent three smale ships for his particular plantation. The greatest whereof being 100 tun. Mr. Reynolds goeth and he with the rest purposeth to come himselfe, for what end I know not.

"The people which they cary are no men for us, wherefore I pray you entertaine them not, neither exchange man for man with them excepte it be some of your worst. He hath taken a patent for himselfe. If they offer to buy anything of you let it be such as you can spare, and let them give the worth of it. If they borrow anything leave a good pawne. . . . I fear these people will not deal so well with the savages as they should. I pray you therefore signifie to Squanto, that they are a distinct body from us, and we have nothing to doe with them, neither can we be blamed for their faults, much less can we warrante their fidelity."

This was the same Weston who in 1622 had established a small colony at Wessagusset, where he had dealt so unfairly with the Indians of the Massachusetts federation that they had planned the uprising of which Massasoit apprised Winslow in March, 1623, and in which they had secured the coöperation of several tribes of the Wampanoag federation, and interested some one of Massasoit's sub-sachems to the extent that he had endeavored to secure his Great Sachem's consent to active participation in the uprising. It was Weston's conduct on this occasion which was responsible for the contemplated attack upon both Wessagusset and Plymouth, the natives not discriminating between them, but, aroused by Weston's outrages, resolved to wipe out the entire white race in New England; and it is characteristic of the methods employed by the colonists to settle such difficulties that they sent Captain Standish to punish the Indians who were concerned in the revolt, which he did; but did nothing to prevent a repetition of the depredations of Weston who had precipitated the trouble.

It was unquestionably the unscrupulous dealings of men like these, covering nearly half a century, that led to many of the complaints; but if the authorities had shown half the zeal in preventing their acts and punishing the offenders that they did in correcting abuses on the part of the Indians, the grievances could easily have been adjusted.

While Philip was under suspicion immediately after Wamsutta's death, it is doubtful whether the authorities had any foundation for the suspicion outside of their own knowledge of wrongdoing on their part and a belief that Philip might avenge the wrongs to his brother and his people. It looks like a case of troubled conscience, resembling that of the small boy who has been guilty of some infraction of parental discipline, and, being out alone after dark, sees lurking in every shadow some fearful agency for the punishment of his misdeeds.

Morton tells us "Metacom made his appearance at the court held at Plymouth, August 6th (1662), did earnestly desire the continuance of that amity and friendship that hath formerly been between the governor of Plymouth and his deceased father and brother." The court thereupon presented articles of agreement which he and his uncle Vucumpowet (Akkompoin) signed.

From that time until 1671, Philip made many concessions by way of land grants that are inexplicable on any other theory than that he was willing to pay any price for peace. He sold parts of Swansea in 1668 and 1669, and all this time he and his people were complaining of their restricted areas. Enough is known of his character to lead to the conclusion that these sales were virtually forced by fear of further acts of vindictive depredation and injustice which he had learned to appreciate as the Englishman's method of securing what he desired, or in the belief that the insatiable greed of the English for land might be finally appeased without crowding his own people completely off the earth.

In 1671 there were further misunderstandings which were adjusted, but from that time on, Philip was constantly under a cloud of suspicion. About this same time, there were rumors of dissatisfaction among the Narragansetts, the young sachems being said to favor war, but the older ones counseling peace, though the commissioners seemed to think that the latter were dissembling, and really favored the resort to arms.   If Philip was actually engaged in an attempt to arouse the Indians to open revolt at that time, he so adroitly baffled their efforts to secure evidence against him that some historians say there isn't a particle of evidence that he ever actually engaged the coöperation of any other tribe.

Matters ran along in this way until the winter of 1674, when John Sassamon, a Massachusetts Indian, who had been educated at Harvard and was an itinerant preacher among the Indians, revealed Philip's plottings to the Plymouth authorities.   He had been employed by Philip as a secretary, and in this way claimed to have secured his information. Knowledge of Sassamon's perfidy reached Philip in some way, and Sassamon suddenly disappeared, and some time later his body was found under the ice in Assawamsett Pond, with the neck broken and other indications of foul play.   Three Indians came under suspicion and they were arrested and indicted by the grand jury.   They were subsequently tried by a jury, and five Indians were called in to hear the evidence against them; and these five concurred in the verdict.   The three were hanged, two of them protesting their innocence.   Philip had been summoned to Plymouth to testify to his connection with the taking off of Sassamon, but did not appear, whether from fear of the consequences or in defiance of the colonists' attempts to subject him to their authority, we can only conjecture.   In any event, the series of depredations that led directly to the war

began immediately after the execution of the men
who were charged with the death of Sassamon.

In connection with the trial of these men one is
constrained to inquire under what authority the
English assumed jurisdiction of this matter. There
is no evidence that Sassamon was subject to them
or under their special protection by reason of any
treaty or agreement. The three men whom they
tried for his murder were Indians, and, if they belonged in the vicinity where the crime was committed, were subjects of the sachem Tuspaquin, and
the offence was against the laws of the territory of
that chief. It was by such acts as this, the utter
ignoring of the rights of the natives to deal with
offenders among their own people against men who
were not subject to the English, and on their own
territory, that the colonists goaded the Indians to
war.

Philip's men limited their depredations to the
killing of the cattle and hogs of the English and
carrying away their property, the purpose apparently being to drive the colonists to the first acts
of violence against the person; and this soon resulted, an Indian being shot and wounded in Swansea, while committing some act of depredation; and
thus the war begun.

July 4, 1675, Captains Moseley and Page, who
were pursuing Philip, received orders to go over
into the Narragansett country and secure a treaty
with the sachems there; and, as a result, they did
succeed in getting a pledge of assistance, signed by
"Agamand, Wampsh, alias Corman, Taitson and

Tawagason, counsellors and attorneys to Canonicus [Pessacus], Ninigret, Matababug, old Quen Quainpen, Quananshet [Canonchet] and Pomham, the six present sachems of the whole Narragansett country." It is significant that not one of the sachems purports to have signed in person; nor is there any evidence that they were present, or that the signatories actually had any authority to sign for them.

About this time, commissioners also attempted to treat with the Nipmucks between the Merrimac and the Connecticut Rivers, but found the young men "surly and insolent," although the old men "showed an inclination for peace." These Nipmucks, the Podunks, who are said to have furnished two hundred warriors, the Nashuas, all the Narragansett sachems except Ninigret, who was really a Niantic, and the Wampanoags, constituted Philip's force, the Narragansetts coming in late in the fall of 1675. It is claimed by some writers that they were under an agreement with Philip to furnish four thousand warriors for an uprising in the spring of 1676, but the death of Sassamon and the execution of his alleged murderers hastened the breaking out of hostilities to such an extent that they did not participate for some months.

From the spring of 1675 until the final overthrow of Philip's forces, no place could feel that it was safe from attack. The towns of Central Massachusetts suffered most severely, the Narragansetts and Wampanoags sweeping up from their territory and joining the Nipmucks and Nashuas in the attacks.

The Indians suffered their first serious defeat in the swamp fight at East Kingston, Rhode Island, December 19, 1675, where three hundred warriors were killed, according to information given by an old squaw who escaped the conflagration caused by the English setting fire to the wigwams, burning women and children. It was at Lancaster on February 10, 1676, that Mary Rowlandson, the minister's wife, and her children were taken in an attack upon that town by the Wampanoags under Philip, Narragansetts under Quinapen and the Nashuas and Nipmucks led by Sagamore Sam and one-eyed John of the Marlborough "praying Indians." She remained a captive for some time, living in the wigwam of Weetamo, who was then one of the squaws of Quinapen; and on one occasion dining with Philip, as she relates in her narrative of her experiences.

Meeting with various reverses, and losing some of their leaders, the Wampanoags and Narragansetts were finally driven into the swamps around Mount Hope in July, 1676. Here the "Old Queen" was slain in that month. It is said that the losses of Philip and his allies amounted to three thousand warriors at that time, but he made another attempt to turn the tide. On July 30, Governor Winslow received word at Marshfield that a strong force was on the march against Taunton or Bridgewater. He hastened to Plymouth, and summoned Captain Church, directing him to rally his forces at once. By this time Philip, apparently seeing the futility of proceeding further, was withdrawing his men.

It was on this retreat, while crossing the river at Taunton on a tree which the Indians had felled to form a bridge, that Akkompoin, the younger brother of Massasoit, was slain with several of his men; and Philip himself came very near meeting the same fate, according to Captain Church, who says that on the morning following Akkompoin's death, he saw an Indian sitting on a log and raised his rifle to fire, when one of his Indians called out that it was a friend, upon which he lowered his gun; and the Indian looked at them and fled. It afterwards turned out to be Philip himself.

Early in August an Indian reported that Philip was at Mount Hope and Church went after him. They came upon him by surprise, and Church aimed at him but his gun missed fire, whereupon he ordered a Seaconnet Indian who was with him to shoot him down. He obeyed, and Philip fell on August 12, 1676, shot through the heart by one of his own people named by the English, John Alderman.

His force was by this time completely shattered, many of his sachems having fallen and others having come in on promises of clemency only to learn that clemency meant either death or slavery as best suited the English. Some of the Nipmucks fled to the west, where they were undoubtedly absorbed by other tribes; and it is said that a remnant of the Wampanoags escaped into Maine where they became merged with the Penobscots.

After Philip's death Church declared that inasmuch as he had caused many Englishmen to remain unburied, no part of him should have burial. An

Indian was summoned who was directed to cut off the head and quarter the body. The head was sent to Plymouth where it was exposed upon a pole for more than a score of years. His hands were sent to Boston, and his quartered body was hung up in the trees where he fell. Church and his men returned to Plymouth "and received their premium, which was thirty shillings per head for the enemies which they had killed or taken, instead of wages. Philip's head went at the same price," according to Captain Church.

The Plymouth clergy celebrated his death with the same blasphemous utterances in which they were wont to give vent to their spleen upon such occasions. The Rev. Increase Mather says: "There was he, like as Agag was hewed in pieces before the Lord, cut into four quarters, and is now hung up as a monument of revenging justice, his head being cut off and carried to Plymouth. So let all thine enemies perish, O Lord! Thus did God break the head of that Leviathan and give it to be meat of the people inheriting the wilderness."

The authorities at Plymouth had appointed a day of thanksgiving for their success. Philip's head reached the town that day. Rev. Cotton Mather says, "God sent 'em in the head of a Leviathan for a thanksgiving feast."

So perished the last of the Great Chiefs of New England to make a stand against the encroachments of the deadly enemies of his people. Of his character much has been written, and the net result of it all is that we know almost nothing concerning

it. Church says he was always the first in flight,
but then proceeds to give the lie to the statement
by saying he was seen sitting on a log at Taunton
River the morning after his uncle and some of his
men were killed. Some writers claim that he possessed no particular skill as an organizer, and
lacked the native eloquence with which some of the
children of the forest roused their followers to
frenzy; while others rank him as a person of great
powers of body and mind, capable of stirring men
to action and not hesitating to risk his own life in
leading his men against the foe. The reader is at
liberty to take his choice; but it may not be amiss
to suggest that such a revolt as he is credited in history with having led does not arise spontaneously,
nor can it be aroused by a man lacking in personal
magnetism, persuasive oratory and physical prowess.
Was he a blood-thirsty savage bent on destruction
of the whites without cause; or was he a true
patriot contending for all that life holds dear, and
sacrificing his own life to the ideals of his race,
freedom, home and the defence of his fatherland?
Undoubtedly most men who have read history have
already drawn their conclusions, and no word of
mine is likely to cause them to change their minds;
but before consigning his name to eternal infamy,
let us look carefully to the conditions surrounding
him, to the grievances of his people, and then let us
ask ourselves what we would have done had we
been in his place. What have men of all races and
of all time done under similar circumstances? and
what appraisal do we place upon their character?

Is there any reason why we should not place Philip of Pokanoket in the class with other men who have made the supreme sacrifice for the maintenance of the same ideals?

Philip married Wootonekanuske, a sister of Weetamo, and believed to be a daughter of Corbitant of the Pocassets, one of the branches of the Wampanoag federation; and, so far as history records, she was his only wife, for while polygamy seems to have been practiced among the Narragansetts in some instances, Quinapen being said by Mrs. Rowlandson to have had three squaws, there is nothing of record to lead to any inference that either Massasoit, Wamsutta or Philip had more than one wife, or that polygamy was ever practiced among the Wampanoags. By her he had two children, one of whom died in infancy, and the other, a young boy at the time of his father's death, was sold with his mother into slavery. The clergy were appealed to by the authorities for their opinion as to what should be done with him, and these followers of Him who said, "Suffer little children to come unto me," were in favor of murdering the child; but the authorities for some reason reserved him for a worse fate and so the grandson of the man who had made their position secure ended his life a slave.

PUMHAM is ranked second to Philip in ability among the leaders of the natives in the uprising. His name appears as one of the six sachems of the Narragansett country in the treaty which Captains Moseley and Page secured from the counsellors in July, 1675. He is spoken of as sachem of Showamet, now Warwick, Rhode Island. In July, 1676, he led an invasion into the territory around Medfield and Dedham, Massachusetts, and on the twenty-fifth of that month, fifty of his band were captured; but he refused to surrender and was shot.

QUINAPEN was a nephew of Miantonomo. After Weetamo left her fourth husband because of his adherence to the English, Quinapen, though much younger than she, took her as the third of his squaws. He was an active participant with his warriors in the various raids by the Narragansetts and is known to have led them in the attack on Lancaster in February, 1676. After his capture in August of that year, he told his captors that he had been second in command at the swamp fight at East Kingston. He was shot at Newport soon after his capture.

CANONCHET, a son of Miantonomo, is referred to as the Chief Sachem of the Narragansetts. He is said to have entered the war with two thousand warriors. Whether this is intended to include the entire strength of the Narragansetts, all of them being in a sense, under his command, or only his own immediate followers is uncertain. Early in the spring of 1676, he and King Philip swept around Seekonk, Massachusetts, with fifteen hundred warriors, and there were six or seven hundred around Pawtucket, Rhode Island, at the same time; but this really throws no light upon the question, because we do not know how many of these were Wampanoags. Canonchet was in command at the swamp fight, with his cousin Quinapen second.

In the raid around Seekonk and Pawtucket in the spring of 1676, he was crossing the Blackstone River, when his foot slipped, throwing him into the water and wetting his gun so that it became useless. This misfortune so disheartened him for the moment that he was easily overtaken by a swift-footed Pequot, who was with a pursuing party of whites and Indians. After his capture, the first Englishman to approach him presented a very youthful appearance. When this young man attempted to interrogate him, he replied, "You much child. No understand matters of war. Let your brother or your chief come. Him I will answer." His capture occurred on March 27th; and he was taken to Stonington, Connecticut, where, after the mockery of a trial, he was first offered his life if he would become an ally of the English. This he steadfastly refused, and when reminded of "his boast that he would not deliver up so much as a paring of a Wampanoag nail when called upon by the English to give up their enemies, and his threat that he would burn them alive in their houses," his courage remained unshaken; and when told that his sentence was death, he stoically replied that it pleased him well that he should die before his heart was soft and he had said anything unworthy of himself. "This," says the devout Hubbard, "was the confusion of a damned wretch that had often opened his mouth to blaspheme the name of the living God and those that make profession thereof," to which he might have truthfully added, but whose practices did not square with their professions; and who worshipped the "living God" with their lips, but blasphemed His name by their every act.

The sentence of the court was carried out in the manner described by Hubbard in the following words: "And that all might share in the glory of destroying so great a prince and come under the obligation of fidelity to each other, the Pequots shot him, the Mohicans cut off his head and quartered his body, and the Ninnicrafts (a name apparently sometimes applied to the Niantics) made the fire and burned his quarters, and as a token of their love and fidelity to the English, presented his head to the counsel of Hartford."

Whether the Pequot traitor to his native land and his people received the thirty pieces of silver for his head, or whether the Connecticut troops and their allies were paid in some other way, we are not told. He fell a victim to the same methods of dealing with the natives that had marked the end of his father, Miantonomo, and at the hands of the same cruel enemies of his nation, acting as the agents of the real enemies of them all, who simply used the Mohicans as their catspaws until such time as it should suit their purpose to destroy them by insidious acts of oppression worse than war. These two men stand, in unbiased history, with Philip, as leaders of their race, who earnestly desired an honorable peace with the whites; and who labored to secure it with the blessings of a higher civilization for their people; but who were swallowed up in the maelstrom of English land covetousness, suspicion and trickery.

TUSPAQUIN has already been referred to as the sachem of the Assawamsetts and probably of the Nemaskets, the two tribes occupying the territory now included in the towns of Lakeville and Middleborough, and parts of Freetown (East), Rochester, and Acushnet. He is commonly referred to as the "Black Sachem." He married Amie, daughter of Massasoit, and had two sons, William and Benjamin. At the outbreak of the war, he joined with his brother-in-law Philip in his attempt to redress by force of arms the grievances of his people, suffered at the hands of the English. William is said to have followed his father, and to have lost his life early in the war, no mention of him appearing after the spring of 1675.

Early in July, 1676, the authorities issued a general proclamation offering clemency to such of their enemies as should come in and give themselves up. Tuspaquin, still adhering to Philip, did not avail himself of this offer; and after the death of Philip, Captain Benjamin Church went looking for him. Church went to Rochester, but was told that he had gone away to the southward; whereupon he took Tuspaquin's wife and children and returned with them to Plymouth, leaving two squaws to tell him what had become of his family and that he would spare all their lives and his too, if he would come down to them and bring the other two that were with him. Church informs us that he was acting upon a commission from Plymouth which authorized him "to receive to mercy, give quarter or not, excepting some particular and noted mur-

derers, viz.: Philip and all that were at the destroying of Mr. Clarke's garrison and some few others."
Tuspaquin does not come within either of these
classes unless it is "some few others"; and the
question naturally arises, if he was in that class, why
did Church promise to spare his life and the lives
of the two others who were with him?

Tuspaquin came in with the two others, and the
authorities, taking advantage of Church's absence
on business in Boston, executed both Tuspaquin and
Annawon to whom Church had given his word that
he would intercede in his behalf. This promise he
faithfully kept, and it was no fault of his that those
in authority broke their promises made through him
to Tuspaquin. Attention should here be called to
the fact that some inducement had been held out
to him beyond the mere promise of clemency, for
we are told that he had "hopes of being made a
captain under Church," but when the authorities
at Plymouth decided upon his execution in Church's
absence, they claimed that "the promise of a captain's place depended upon his being impenetrable
by bullets, a claim that the Indians had made for
him." So in order to put him to the test they confronted him with a firing squad with the result that
we would expect; but which their pious historians
exploit with great gusto, probably meaning to infer
that he was not executed, but was merely being
tried out to determine whether he met with the
requirements for a captaincy. They conclude with
a statement that he was found to be penetrable by
the English guns, for he fell down at the first shot

and thereby received the "just reward for his wickedness." Was he shot as a "reward for his wickedness," or to test the question of his impenetrability? If there is any one thing for which the early writers were more noted than for another, it is not consistency. That this claim was merely a subterfuge under which the English sought to cloak their perfidy must be perfectly apparent to the discerning reader.

ANNAWON, the last of Philip's great captains, is spoken of by Schoolcraft as an uncle of Philip, but I find nothing in the writings of historians of the early period to warrant the belief that he was in any way related to the royal family of the Pokanokets, and in boasting of his prowess after his capture, he speaks of Massasoit simply as Philip's father. This is not by any means conclusive, however, as we have no knowledge of Massasoit's wife, and Annawon may well have been her brother. If there is anything in the early history to establish this fact or to lead to any inference that it is a fact, I have not found it. There is no doubt that he was one of Massasoit's counsellors and "men of valor," and he may have been related to him by blood or marriage.

At the fight in the swamp below Mount Hope, immediately following Philip's death, the English plainly heard some one shouting, "Iootash! Iootash!" ("Stand firm! Stand firm!") On inquiry of some of their Indian allies, the English were told that this was Old Annawon, Philip's captain. With the faithful few of the Wampanoags who refused to take advantage of the English offers of clemency or of the opportunities for flight to distant lands, Annawon made his way into Rehoboth, Massachusetts, where they constructed a rude shelter by felling trees against the perpendicular side of a ledge that extends a distance of about seventy-five feet, at a height of about twenty-five feet in its highest place, a short distance from the highway running from Taunton to Providence.   Some of his men who were out on a foraging party were discovered and followed by Captain Church, who recites in detail the manner of his capture.   He tells of lowering himself down from the top of the rock to the level of the camp by clinging to the branches of the trees; but as the distance from the top of the rock to the level of the shelter is only about six feet at that place, and easily traversed, this looks like some of Church's exploitation of his personal prowess.   The ledge where he was captured has ever since been known as "Annawon's Rock."   After his surprise and capture, while Church and Annawon were lying side by side to rest for the night, the latter suddenly arose and walked away, Church not molesting him.   After some time, he returned and laid down a quantity of wampum and Philip's personal belongings, saying they had been his king's, but as they had killed the king, he supposed they belonged to the English.

If there was any foundation for Annawon's claim that he had been a mighty warrior and had performed deeds of valor "when serving under Philip's father," it is apparent that he must have been an

old man at that time. Massasoit was not engaged
in any wars that called for heroic exploits after
1620, and probably none after the decimation of his
tribe by the plague in 1616 or 1617, unless it was
the war with the Narragansetts which resulted in
the loss to them of Aquidnick. Indian youths were
not trained for war until they were eighteen, and
so Annawon must have been born around 1600 or
before. At any rate he was old enough not to be a
menace to the whites with all his warriors gone, and
the only explanation of his execution is in the words
used by the English in their characterization of the
Indians. Cruel, blood-thirsty vindictiveness is the
only answer to the question, Why did they refuse to
listen to the plea of Church for leniency, and shoot
this old man who was on the verge of the grave?
What became of the small band that was captured
with him including his son, we are not told, but
from what we know of the colonists' methods, it is
not difficult for us to see them in fancy wearing out
their lives and fretting away their freeborn spirits
under the slave drivers' lash in the West Indies.

The "Iootash" of old Annawon still rings in our
ears as the last defiant cry of a people who dreamed
of a life of peace and harmony with the strangers
from across the great waters; but who, after half a
century of devotion to the work of bringing about
the realization of their dream, were rudely awakened
to the futility of attempting to reconcile the different
ideals, different manners of living, different customs,
different codes of honor and different stages of progress of the two races; and to the fact that the

attempt was bound to result in virtual vassalage for the less advanced.

I speak of different ideals; but, while it is true that the two races were widely separated in many respects, a careful analysis of the cause for which the red men fought shows that they made the supreme sacrifice for much the same ideals that actuated the whites in their struggles for freedom. They were contending for liberty, justice and equality, the liberty they enjoyed before the white man came, justice at the hands of the men whose enterprise they had aided, in their dealings with them, and equality with the colonists in the enjoyment of that liberty and the administration of that justice.

And so the "Iootash" of Annawon was nothing more nor less than an appeal to his handful of followers to stand firm for the ideals which we are accustomed to call "American," and which are American in a broader sense than we apply the term, because they were the ideals of the first Americans of whom we have any definite knowledge.

Annawon stood firm for the protection of the families and homes of his people, for the graves of his fathers and the freedom of his hunting grounds; and out of respect to the memory of his race and his valiant band, the last of the tribe of Massasoit, this work has been prepared, in the hope that it may aid in awakening a spirit of justice and fair play on the part of the sons of their exterminators that shall stand firm for a proper appreciation of their character as the early defenders of the principles we cherish; and of the part their friendship for the colonists, in the days of their weakness, played in laying the foundation upon which succeeding generations have established what we are pleased to call the American Ideal.

The blind, unreasoning suspicion and hate of an earlier age ruthlessly and needlessly crushed the hopes and aspirations of a once free and friendly people beneath the cornerstone of the structure, and stained it with the lifeblood of a race. We cannot wipe away the stain, but we may avoid participation in the sins of the fathers, and make atonement for them, by standing firm for the ideals for which the children of nature, as well as the sons of their destroyers, have shed their blood; and by giving to the aborigines the meed of honor which is their due. Let them take their place in history beside the men of other races and other climes who have struggled against the forces which would sweep them away; who have fearlessly bared their breasts in defence of their freedom and the right to transmit it to their posterity.

The man dies, but the memory of his deeds remains as a priceless heritage to those who come after him; and the last defiant cry of Annawon to his followers is his contribution to history, his legacy to the world. In the cause of his ideals and ours, humanity calls to us to hear and heed the cry, "Iootash!"

www.ingramcontent.com/pod-product-compliance
Lightning Source LLC
Chambersburg PA
CBHW061719270326
41928CB00011B/2036